AMERICA
IS BETTER
THAN THIS

AMERICA IS BETTER THAN THIS

TRUMP'S WAR AGAINST MIGRANT FAMILIES

SENATOR JEFF MERKLEY

TWELVE

NEW YORK   BOSTON

Twelve
Hachette Book Group
1290 Avenue of the Americas, New York, NY 10104
twelvebooks.com

twitter.com/twelvebooks

First Edition: August 2019

Twelve is an imprint of Grand Central Publishing. The Twelve name and logo are trademarks of Hachette Book Group, Inc.

The publisher is not responsible for websites (or their content) that are not owned by the publisher.

The Hachette Speakers Bureau provides a wide range of authors for speaking events. To find out more, go to www.hachettespeakersbureau.com or call (866) 376-6591.

Library of Congress Control Number: 2019941774

ISBNs: 978-1-5387-3419-3 (hardcover), 978-1-5387-3418-6 (ebook)

Printed in the United States of America

LSC-C

10 9 8 7 6 5 4 3 2 1

I dedicate this book to Yaquelin, Andrea, and Carolina, and to all the migrant children who have arrived at our border only to find that Lady Liberty's torch has been snuffed out; and in respectful memory of those migrant children who, like Jakelin and Felipe, died at journey's end.

They deserved much better.

TABLE OF CONTENTS

AMERICA
IS BETTER
THAN THIS

PROLOGUE

The Most Cruel Law

THE STATE OF THE UNION IS ONE OF THE BIGGEST EVENTS OF the year on Capitol Hill. On that day the most powerful people in Washington gather, alongside the nation's media, to take stock of where we are as a nation, and where we're headed. On that self-important night in early 2019, amid all the Senators and Supreme Court Justices, all the TV reporters and celebrity guests, were two humble young women from Guatemala: Albertina and Yaquelin Contreras.[1] For most newcomers to the grand marble hallways of Congress, the sights and sounds can be overwhelming. But for this mother and daughter, the change in their surroundings and circumstances were even more striking.

Albertina and Yaquelin are survivors of President Donald Trump's devastating child separation policy. They came to Capitol Hill to share their story, to bear witness to the brutality of child separation, and to encourage President Trump and Congress to treat refugees seeking asylum with the dignity and respect that all human beings deserve.

Just nine months earlier they had left their home in the small town of Cubulco, about four hours' drive north of the Guatemalan capital, to escape horrific sexual violence. A rape survivor herself, Albertina was terrified that her eleven-year-old daughter was also going to become a target as she grew into a teenager. After all, she was just a teenager herself when she gave birth to Yaquelin. Either the local street gang would force her daughter to become a sex slave, or she would be collecting extortion cash for the gang. If they refused, the gang would simply kill one of them. If they complied, her daughter faced a future of rape and beatings just like her own. The decision to leave was painful. She could save only one of her three children. So she chose the most vulnerable, leaving behind her two sons, who are just four and nine years old, with her sister.

They borrowed the cash to pay the smugglers: $6,500 for the two of them to travel north, through the exhaustion, hunger, and the constant fear of the drug cartels, before reaching the bridge over the Rio Grande that is the border crossing between Ciudad Juárez, Mexico, and El Paso, Texas. They tried three times to enter the United States to claim asylum, but guards would stop them in the middle of the bridge.

"They told us the bridge is only there for people crossing legally," she told me. "So we were forced to find another place to cross into the United States."

Going back to Guatemala was not an option: The local gang knew they had defied them by leaving, and their return would only make them a target of violence and extortion.

The gangs do not want their neighbors to know that anyone can simply leave to escape their reign of terror.

But as they tried to find another way across the border, they were abducted by another cartel. For hours they thought they were going to die. If you don't pay the coyotes additional cash, your choices are very limited if you want to survive. Albertina and Yaquelin have never told the story of what happened in those hours. All they would say is that they were barely alive: It was as if they were dead already.[2]

Albertina and Yaquelin finally crossed the Rio Grande on their own and were immediately arrested by Border Patrol officers. "You're animals" were the first words they heard when they set foot in the United States. "We don't want to see more immigrants here."

That was when they faced an entirely new and unexpected horror. For eight hours they were confined in an ice-cold holding cell, known to migrants as *una hielera*—an icebox—with just a space blanket to keep them warm. Then came the official interview for the twenty-seven-year-old mother and her eleven-year-old daughter.

"We did the interview and one of the men told me we're going to be separated and that I was going to prison to pay for the crime of coming here," she said. "I never expected they would separate children from parents. As a mother, that was something I never expected. It was cruel."

Her daughter watched as they shackled her mother's wrists, ankles, and waist, and took her away. "All I could think was how sad it was," said Yaquelin. "My mother wasn't a criminal. All she was trying to do was find a way to give me a better future."

For two months they knew nothing about each other's condition or location. Albertina was sent to El Paso county jail, which she described as "a place of terror," where she was kept in solitary confinement for roughly a week. Her daughter was sent to a detention center with other girls separated from their parents. "All the girls worried about what would happen to our parents," she said. "We all cried."

Albertina was released on the same day a judge ordered the immediate end to Trump's policy of ripping children away from their parents, as well as the rapid reunification of families. But Yaquelin was 800 miles away at a child prison run by a government contractor in San Benito, Texas, in the Rio Grande Valley. Trump officials initially refused to reunite her with her mother, saying that Albertina needed to pass what they called a "parental fitness assessment." Albertina moved to a town near Nashville, Tennessee, and with the help of a pro bono lawyer, she challenged their decision and won her daughter's release.

Eventually they were reunited at the Nashville airport, and a group of well-wishers gave them the welcome they deserved.

Now, six months after their reunion, they were my special guests in Washington, sitting in the same House chamber where the man who separated them would be speaking to the nation.

I asked them: If they could tell Donald Trump one thing, what would they say?

"Separating kids from parents is the most cruel law I have ever seen," said Yaquelin. "It's not just. It's not right that we were treated this way."

* * *

This "most cruel" law, Trump's child separation policy, makes me think about terrible situations around the world in which children are the targets or the victims. I've witnessed a number of them. I'll never forget meeting three mothers from Sudan at a refugee camp in Kenya. Each carried her baby. One baby was dying of malaria. A second was dying of AIDS. The third was dying of malnutrition. Nor can I forget visiting a room of women at a refugee camp in Bangladesh, who told me how the Burmese government had burned their homes down around them, killed their children and husbands, and raped them and their daughters.

But the horror of child separation is not some evil perpetrated in a vicious civil war or a national campaign of genocide by a dictator in some far-off land.

It is here, in America. It is perpetrated by our government, with our resources, on our land. It is the centerpiece of Trump's war on migrant children. Trump's war includes child separation, cages, family internment camps, border blockades, and a network of child prisons on American soil that as of December 2018 held 15,000 migrant children.

If this was happening somewhere else, we would shake our heads in disbelief. Congress would pass resolutions condemning the policy and the practice. Human rights leaders would call for economic sanctions or boycotts. We would all wonder how any nation could go so far off track.

But this travesty is here, in our nation. Our beloved United States of America. Even if some people refuse to believe it—even if it sounds too shocking to be true—we need to confront the reality of what Donald Trump and his administration have done in the name of the American people. No one else will fix this. This responsibility is ours. We in America must be the ones to shine a light on it, and put an end to it.

This issue is deeply personal for me. I was raised to believe in the great American enterprise of equality and opportunity for all, and to believe that every individual merits being treated with respect and dignity. When my government, with my tax money, deliberately injures migrant children, I am going to fight to defend those children in every way I can. When my government lies to the American people, I am going to seek to share the truth.

We, the American people, must not stand idle while this profound injustice continues. Let us use all the power inherent in our "We the People" republic to restore accountability and decency.

America is better than this!

ONE

CHILD SEPARATION

ON A SUNNY DAY IN MAY 2018, U.S. ATTORNEY GENERAL JEFF Sessions traveled to the fenced beach that separates San Diego, California, from Tijuana, Mexico. He spoke from behind a large round seal of the Department of Homeland Security mounted on a stocky wooden lectern, against the backdrop of the high, slatted steel bars of the border fence that slices through the sand and dips toward the ocean.

He was speaking just outside a unique meeting place for Mexicans and Americans, called Friendship Park, dedicated as a national monument in 1971 by first lady Pat Nixon. For two decades, there was nothing more than an international line separating the two countries. Then came a fence, the 9/11 attacks, and the park was closed to the public. Eventually there came a second fence, closing off the park except under strict official control. Friendship was fenced in.

Standing next to Thomas Homan, the Acting Director of Immigration and Customs Enforcement (ICE), Sessions sounded like he thought the United States was under attack: "Today we are here to send a message to the world: we are not going to let this country be overwhelmed. People are not going to caravan or otherwise stampede our border."

Sessions quickly went on to say that meant "100 percent of illegal southwest border crossings" would be prosecuted. What had been a violation of civil law was now going to be a crime. "I have put in place a 'zero tolerance' policy for illegal entry on our southwest border," he said. "If you cross this border unlawfully, then we will prosecute you. It's that simple. If you smuggle illegal aliens across our border, then we will prosecute you. If you are smuggling a child, then we will prosecute you and that child will be separated from you as required by law."[1]

My eyes widened. Trump's new policy had a catchy name, "Zero Tolerance," that made it seem like a get-tough-on-crime doctrine, but the details sounded like something altogether different. This was a policy that marked refugees as criminals for the "crime" of fleeing oppression. Moreover, a central feature was that children would be torn from their parents' arms before the adults would be locked up in prison indefinitely.

I was astounded. How would our nation be different today if our ancestors fleeing persecution abroad had been treated as criminals in the past? And how would our nation be different if our ancestors who were brought here by force or subterfuge, from African slaves to indentured Chinese workers, had been received with freedom and opportunity?

I thought about how scary it is for children to flee the familiar surroundings of their land on a perilous journey to a new place with a different culture and different language, and how the only thing that gives a child some sense of confidence and stability is the trust he or she has in the parent and the ability to hold the father's or mother's hand. And now Sessions and Trump were proposing to rip that hand away, leaving the children with no understanding of why their parents had abandoned them and no sense of what would become of them. The children would be locked up in a system of expanding child prisons.

How different this is from the vision of America inscribed on the Statue of Liberty as a welcoming home for "your tired, your poor, your huddled masses yearning to breathe free." Trump's and Sessions' new policy demolishes the notion that we are a nation that treats people fleeing persecution with fundamental respect and dignity.

The core of this new policy seemed to be the infliction of massive trauma on children. This "Zero Tolerance" policy sounded more like "Zero Humanity."

I refused to believe that the Trump administration really planned to implement this policy. Surely, here in the land of Lady Liberty, with her torch held high to light the way for refugees, Trump was not planning to criminalize a flight from oppression and inflict harm on children.

Therefore, I concluded, Sessions' announcement of Trump's new policy must be more rhetoric than reality. No matter how tough the Trump administration wanted to sound on immigration, I couldn't believe that they would establish an immigration policy based on deliberately hurting children.

I shared my thoughts with my team. "They can't possibly be doing this," I said.

One member of my team, Lauren Oppenheimer, responded with the words that set me out on a journey: "There is one way to find out, and that is to go to the border."

She was right. I had to go to the border to find out.

* * *

The first Sunday of June 2018, I was on a plane headed for McAllen, Texas, via Houston. My trip got off to a rough start. I hit a travel delay in Houston when the plane's air-conditioning broke, and we sat sweating on the tarmac while the airline rustled up a replacement plane. This delay crunched an already short trip, making it impossible to visit the border bridge that connects across the Rio Grande to Reynosa, Mexico.

When I landed, Jennifer Harbury, a volunteer assisting the migrants, filled me on what I missed. She had witnessed fifty or more migrants stranded on the American side of the bridge because they had been refused entry through the doors of the U.S. port of entry building at the foot of the bridge. They were afraid to go back to Reynosa because of the gangs that would prey on them. Jennifer had been ferrying food and water to the migrants, some of who had been there in the heat for as long as ten days. Now the bridge would have to wait for another visit.

Twenty minutes' drive from the international bridge is a neighborhood of single-story industrial units and warehouses. There, in an otherwise unremarkable building, Customs and Border Protection (CBP) detains and interviews migrants to determine their fate.

That was our first stop, and our delay in arriving did have one advantage. It introduced an element of surprise into our visit. According to the immigration advocates, buses had transported a lot of immigrants away shortly before we were to arrive, which would of course make the place look less crowded and more organized. But during the delay, Border Patrol agents had brought in more migrants, filling it up again. We would get a more authentic look at their operation.

Upon arrival I found a sizable press huddle across the street from the compound. Ray Zaccaro, my Senate Communications Director, had alerted some press to my visit, but I never anticipated that there would be such substantial interest.

"What's going on inside?" asked one local reporter.

"None of you have been allowed inside?" I replied, surprised to hear that the media was excluded from such an important place. "Well, I'll go inside and see, and tell you what's going on after I come out. Because I have no idea what they are doing."

In America, it's never a good sign when the press has been barred entry to see the basic operations of our government. The press had not been let in for a simple reason: The Trump administration did not want the press, and by extension the American people, to see how they were treating immigrants.

Walking out of the briefing room to the holding cells, I was stunned by what I saw.

Stuffed inside what looked like dog kennels were dozens of people. On the left and right were pens divided by cinder block walls, with fencing across the front. Men in the pens on the left, women and children on the right. These are the *hieleras*, the notorious holding cells that the CBP often keeps cold to make life miserable for refugees.

The pens were jammed with humanity. Some migrants were trying to lie down but there simply wasn't enough room, so several were sitting with their knees up. They were wrapped in Mylar space blankets and had nothing but the clothes on their backs. At the back of each pen was a low wall that served as a half-screen for a toilet. The migrants looked terrified, and many of the women were crying.

Beyond the holding pens was a room with computer stations where new immigrants were being interviewed through a live video link with an officer elsewhere. At that moment there was a family lined up with a teenage girl in front of them speaking into a video station.

"What's going on here?" I asked. "Does this girl belong with the family? And why is she being interviewed instead of the father?"

The officials explained they interviewed the family members separately to see if their stories matched up, to figure out whether they really were a family.

We stepped from the interview room into a large warehouse-style space. It was filled with thirty-foot-square chain-linked cages, separating adults from children, men from women, and boys from girls. It was disturbingly quiet for a room with so many people held inside.

The CBP officials wanted to show us where the food was prepared for their detainees, but I told them I wasn't interested. Then they offered to show us the medical center and the first aid supplies, but I was fixated by those chain-link cages.

"I don't want to see your medical facility," I said. "I want to know about these people in these cages."

The pens and cages were not new construction. Their existence and use had preceded the Trump administration. The issue was how they were being used to implement Trump's child separation strategy.

They had pulled a young father and teenage son out of the cages, saying they had just reunited them. It appeared to be a moment that was staged for us, and they asked the father how he and his son were doing. The father said they were fine, but his eyes told another story. He looked for all the world like he was trapped in a world he didn't understand and feared for his fate.

We stopped at a cage in the center of the warehouse where a couple dozen boys were held. They were lining up by height, waiting to be fed. The smallest and youngest looked knee-high to a grasshopper, about four years old.

"So have these children, these boys, been separated from their parents?" I asked.

"Well, not all of them have been separated," the officer said.

"So some came by themselves to the border?"

"Yes, some of the older ones came by themselves."

"But some of these kids were separated from their parents?"

"Yes," the officer answered.

"Well, where do you do that?" I asked in disbelief. I couldn't get my head around what was taking place. He pointed to the door we had just passed through.

"We bring them in through that door, and that's where we separate them."

Child separation. There it was, right in front of me. I was soon to learn, and the nation was soon to learn, that under Zero Tolerance the CBP was forcibly taking more than a thousand kids a month from their parents. The separations happened at various stages. Some at the border, some at the *hieleras*, some at the processing centers. The separations happened in different ways. Some children were torn out of their parents' arms. Some were led away under a ruse of a medical check or a meal or a bathroom break, never to return. Some parents were told their children were being taken. Others were told they would soon be reunited.

No matter how it was done, it was horrific. Desperate parents. Desperate and disturbed children. Neither the parents nor the children having any idea of how the system works, and when or if they would ever see their children again.

Back in the warehouse, standing in front of the cage of boys, I looked around. Through the chain-link fences you could make out some of the groups of adults. I wondered how long the boys would be in that cage before they were whisked away. And whether they could catch glimpses of their mothers or fathers or sisters, and whether it would be the last glimpse they would have for a very long time.

I am generally an even-keeled person. But I was stunned and angry at what I had just witnessed. As we left the building, Ray Zaccaro, my Communications Director, looked emotionally distraught. "I can't believe what we just saw," he said.

As promised, I spoke to the handful of local reporters and cameras outside and described what I had just seen. It was an emotional hour, but more was to come.

*   *   *

Before seeing *las hieleras* and the warehouse cages, the CBP officials had set Ray and me down in a briefing room. They were determined to give us the official story, complete with diagrams and charts, seated around long white tables like a classroom. They cited statistics and even showed us a promotional video. I was impatient.

I asked the lead officer, Lloyd Easterling, division chief for the CBP, Rio Grande Valley, if they were separating children from their parents, as envisioned by Sessions' and Trump's Zero Tolerance policy. He admitted they were splitting families apart.

"Well, are you comfortable doing that, given the potential trauma to the children?"

There was a long silence.

"We don't make the policies," Chief Easterling finally replied. "It's our job to implement them."

I pressed on. "I've read that when you separate the kids it's hard for the parents to find their kids and the kids to find their parents."

"Oh no, that's not true," he assured me. "They all have A-numbers."

"So the kids have the A-numbers of their parents and the parents have the A-numbers of their kids?"

He responded that that was exactly right.

A-numbers are alien registration numbers that are up to nine digits long. The CBP officials said they gave the A-numbers to migrants on a piece of paper that also had a phone number migrants could call to find family members. I'm not sure how they thought migrants would keep track of the paper with their own A-number—let alone the A-numbers for their family members—as the CBP moved them from place to place in the immigration system. The numbers weren't on a wrist band or neck chain they could easily track. And the numbers were way too long to memorize.

The system for keeping families connected seemed flawed, so I explored it further.

"Are you saying this works really well? That a parent or child can call this number and easily find their family member?"

He insisted it worked superbly. I decided to give them one more chance to square their answer with the reports that migrant parents were having great difficulty finding their children, let alone reaching them on the telephone.

"Maybe what you're saying is that it works really well in theory, but would you acknowledge there are some problems in implementation? Some kinks to get worked out?"

They would acknowledge no such thing. One officer responded: "It works really well in practice."

As I strongly suspected then, and was confirmed later, the system didn't work as billed. The parents were held by the Department of Homeland Security (DHS). DHS transferred the separated children to the Office of Refugee Resettlement (ORR) in the Department of Health and Human Services. The two agencies had completely different computer systems.

And when DHS separated the kids from their parents, they reclassified the children as Unaccompanied Alien Children (UACs). So ORR had no idea which UACs truly arrived at the border unaccompanied and which UACs were children who had arrived with parents. The ORR computers did not have the parents' names in the file with the child's name.

Little to no planning had gone into keeping track of the families as a whole. And there were operational problems that were highlighted when I joined other Oregon members of Congress weeks later, visiting parents held at a federal prison in Sheridan, Oregon. They pointed out that when they arrived at the prison, the prison authorities had taken away their papers. So if they had ever had a paper with an A-number, they didn't have it now. They were being held in their cells for most of the day to keep them separated from the regular inmates at the prison, so they had little opportunity to access a phone. In addition, they pointed out that the phone cost money to use and they didn't have any money.

There was in theory a free phone number, but most didn't know about it. And some who did and tried the phone, found out that no one on the other end of the line spoke their language. Although many migrants speak Spanish, others from Central America speak indigenous languages. And yet other migrants, like the ones we were meeting with, were from other parts of the world. It is hard to get a facilitator on the line who could communicate with the migrants from countries as diverse as Bangladesh, Brazil, Mauritania, and Congo.

If the adults couldn't make the system work, there was no way their children were going to make it work. While a few parents found their children through the persistence of helpful staff or volunteers, for most it was as if they were imprisoned on separate planets.

It was clear to me from Easterling's response to my inquiries that I was going to get the glossy "everything is perfect and wonderful" treatment, not honest evaluations of the strengths and weaknesses of the system.

A DHS Inspector General report issued in September 2018, confirmed the problem I was asking about.[2] DHS "struggled to identify, track, and reunify families separated under Zero Tolerance due to limitations with its information technology systems, including a lack of integration between systems." The report summary continued, "DHS provided inconsistent information to aliens who arrived with children during Zero Tolerance, which resulted in some parents not understanding that they would be separated from their children, and being unable to communicate with their children after separation."

* * *

Upon leaving the CBP processing center, we headed for a humanitarian respite center for new immigrants, run by the Sacred Heart sisters. Even after the start of Zero Tolerance, the CBP was not locking up all the migrants who had crossed the border. They just didn't have enough space. So CBP officials would take a group of migrants and dump them onto the street near the respite center without money or food or a plan on where to go. That puts migrants in a pretty desperate condition. Fortunately, the Sacred Heart team stepped in to help.

The center was packed. Some migrants were sitting on chairs, some on the floor. Some simply stood as they waited for help. It wasn't clear where they would go or how they would fend for themselves. The volunteers at the shelter would assist each migrant by sitting with them, listening to them, getting them food, helping them figure out a plan, and working to put them in contact with family or friends who could provide a room and a bus ticket.

I began asking a few of them about the warehouse, especially how long they had been there. Children are supposed to be detained there no more than 72 hours, but the new arrivals at the respite center said some children were being held for more than a week.

I sat down to speak to a pregnant woman and asked where she was going to go. The staff were helping her figure out what relative she was going to stay with, and how she would get the money for a bus ticket. I asked why she came to the United States, and her answer was a punch to the stomach. "I was gang-raped," she said. "That's why I left."

* * *

Our next planned stop was a former Walmart store in Brownsville, about an hour away. This was a child prison run by Southwest Key Programs. I had heard that as many as 1,000 boys might be stuck inside there. That sounded impossible, but worth checking out.

My staff had sought official permission to visit, but the Office of Refugee Resettlement (ORR) had rejected our request, saying that two weeks' notice was required. That seemed over the top. It made planning very difficult, given complex congressional schedules. And it surely didn't take two weeks for ORR to arrange for an on-site manager to show one around. There are two main reasons, in my mind, for this policy. The first is to discourage members of Congress from visiting. The second is to give them plenty of time to implement the Potemkin Village strategy of making a place look perfect before a visit. Neither reason is acceptable.

ORR does have the ability to waive the two-week requirement, and we asked for a waiver. ORR had turned us down. So Ray asked me if we should still go. It was a long way. It was hot out. And they probably weren't going to let us in the door.

"You know what? Yes. Let's go," I said. "I'll knock on the door. I'll introduce myself and ask if there's someone to show me around. It's a large facility. They might show us because we are there, and it's not that big a deal to walk us around."

We drove on to Brownsville in our rented black Nissan Altima, with a handful of local reporters tagging along in their own cars. We were hot, tired, and hungry, but we also knew we were beginning to see something that no outsider had witnessed. On the way there I recorded a video to post to Facebook, telling everyone what we had seen in McAllen and what we were hoping to see in Brownsville. In a democracy, we need to ask questions and we need to expect answers. So we were heading to this facility in Brownsville to do just that.

Southwest Key calls this facility a shelter. I call it a child prison. I call it a prison because children are sent there and locked up against their will. That sounds more like a prison than a shelter to me. This particular child prison is named Casa Padre, as declared by a large sign above the entry. Translated, that means "Father's House," which is a curious name for a place housing many children who have been forcibly taken from their parents.

In the former Walmart's parking lot, there were a couple of temporary wooden barriers constructed like saw horses, painted with the words KEEP OUT. It appeared that they were designed to keep away cars not associated with Southwest

Key, so we left our Altima farther away and walked past the barriers toward the main door. We started recording another video for Facebook and the media to make sure the world could experience what we were witnessing in real time.

"I think it's unacceptable that a member of Congress is not being admitted to see what is happening to children whose families are applying for asylum," I told the cameras. "So I decided to come out here, and go up to the door, and explain why I'm here, and ask to be let in. So that's what I'm going to do now. Here we go."

As we walked through the parking lot, I talked about my experience in McAllen and the trauma inflicted on children who were separated from their parents there. I explained how this new policy of child separation was meant to assault and hurt these children, supposedly to discourage others from coming. "I think that is a horrific attitude for the United States," I said as I arrived at the main door. "Instead of protecting children as we have always done, and do the best thing for children, instead we're going to proceed to inflict harm on them as a strategy of deterring people from seeking to come to the U.S. following calamity abroad."

The door was shut but there was a piece of paper taped to the blacked-out doorway with a phone number on it, so I called it with my cell phone and put the call on speakerphone. There was no reply, but a detention center worker walked in at that moment. I asked if I could enter with him, but he said I couldn't, that this was private property. I explained I was a member of Congress, and he said no. I asked to speak to a supervisor, and he said there was no one who would approve that.

"I want to know if they have second thoughts about being partners in a process of ripping children away from their families under this new policy," I said to the audience watching on Facebook. "Because it would seem to me that the very good people who run this nonprofit and are dedicated to helping children would not want to be part of an operation that is actually hurting those children."

I tried the phone number again to see if anyone would answer. They picked up and I announced myself. The person answering said she would talk to her supervisor, and I gave her my number live on Facebook. It's not every day you hear a senator's phone number on the internet, but we never thought many people would see the video. Besides, I just wanted to get into the building to see what was happening to those children. It would take me weeks to regain control of my voice mail.

We waited several more minutes and I called for the supervisor again. "I already gave him the message and he left," said the person answering again. At that moment, the local police drove up and sure enough, the supervisor emerged.

"I'll be with you guys in just a minute," the supervisor said as he walked right past me to greet the police officers. On the back of his black T-shirt were the words TEAMWORK MAKES THE DREAM WORK.

That's interesting, I thought. He's not even willing to talk to me about the facility while we are standing in the parking lot. They really didn't want people to know what is going on in this place. All the more reason for members of Congress to exercise some oversight.

It was unnerving to see the police roll up. It never occurred to me that Southwest Key would call them. But I wasn't too worried, in part because I felt I had a certain amount of protection as a U.S. senator. It seemed unlikely that they would slam me to the ground and cuff me, but then again, who could be sure?

I understood his plan: He was never going to talk to me about what was going on behind closed doors with so many millions of taxpayer dollars. But that didn't stop me from asking him what it was like being part of this new policy of family separation. So I asked. He said he couldn't make a statement and instead gave me a number to call in Washington, D.C. Another staff member was pressing the police to force us to leave and to stop the cameras from filming the whole scene. I walked up to the police and explained who I was and why I was there. I recounted that the woman on the phone had said the supervisor would come talk to me, so that's what we were doing. "I'm not allowed to," said the supervisor. "She was misinformed."

The two young police officers were polite: They didn't tell me to leave or try to arrest me.

"I haven't been asked to leave the property but I'm guessing that's about what's going to happen," I said.

"Yes. That's where they're going towards," one of the officers said, before asking me for my name and date of birth. I explained to him that children separated from their families were being detained here. I told the cameras that we still hadn't been asked to leave, and it was only then—when the supervisor overheard me talking—that he did so. I walked up to him, shook his hand, and thanked him.

"I do appreciate the mission that you're all working on. But I think you do have to wrestle with this situation of these children being ripped out of their parents' arms," I said, as he turned his back and walked away.

We had no idea how the Facebook video would travel. We had no idea how many people were astonished by the secrecy and the reality of the Trump administration's war on migrant families. That video was viewed more than 2 million times and shared by more than forty thousand people.

We left the parking lot and went for dinner nearby with one of our friends from the ACLU in Texas, Michael Seifert. Michael has worked with the border communities for many decades, arriving in the Rio Grande Valley as a Catholic priest. He first worked with the ACLU when the State Department began denying passports to U.S. citizens in his parish, based on the notion that midwives were issuing supposedly fraudulent birth certificates. Now he was working full time for the ACLU as a border advocacy strategist in Brownsville, living just half a mile from the border.

He took us to a restaurant called El Ultimo Taco, where the beer and tacos were delicious. The place was so warm and welcoming, it felt like the best way to recover from a day that had drained us. In a simple restaurant, where people of all heritages are eating together, it is hard to find what separates us as people living in the same part of the world. We were trying to digest the day, to make sense of what we had experienced; trying to understand why anyone would want to hurt these families so much.

On our way back to our hotel near McAllen, I took the wheel to let Ray catch up on his emails and messages.

"I'm glad we went to Brownsville," I said.

"I'm glad you didn't listen to me," he replied.

*   *   *

When we drove down the road to Brownsville we had no idea how our visit would play out, or how bright a spotlight it would put on Trump's policy of child separation, or how viscerally the American people would react.

Two major things caught the public's attention. One was children being sorted into cages at the processing center. Those cages became a vivid symbol for the brutality of child separation. The second was the secrecy surrounding the former Walmart in Brownsville. People figured if the Trump administration was that keen to block access, the story was not going to be a good one.

For what it's worth, the fact-checkers at the *Washington Post* were not impressed when I called the chain-link fence enclosures at the processing center "cages." They gave me several Pinocchios for inaccuracy. How ironic that in the age where virtually nothing Trump says is accurate, the *Post* criticized my honest description of what those enclosures looked like. It gives me some satisfaction that after the press and other members of Congress visited the facility, everyone calls them cages.

In a double whammy, the *Post* also gave me Pinocchios for saying that ORR had a policy of making it difficult for members of Congress to see how these facilities are operating. I stand by my statement. A two-week advance requirement for planning a visit is all about making it hard for members to schedule a visit and hard for them to see how a facility is actually operating before it is cleaned up to give the best— and possibly very misleading—impression.

"I just don't feel that any member of Congress should have to wait weeks or months to visit a facility to see what the hell is going on inside of it," I told *Time* magazine. "They're trying to wrap this in a blanket of secrecy."[3]

A spokesperson for Trump's Department of Health and Human Services (HHS) stated that "thankfully for the safety, security, and dignity of the children being cared for there, they were denied access."[4] The argument that the government is "protecting" children has become the universal defense for unsavory policies and procedures that hurt children. Tyler Houlton, a press secretary for the Department of Homeland Security, echoed this theme: "Contrary to any misinformation campaign, the safety of children is paramount for DHS."[5]

If only those same officials were as concerned about the mental health of those children as they were about their "dignity." Of course, they were only following the lead of Trump himself, who blamed everyone else for his own cruelty to children. His favorite strategy has been to blame the law and the Democrats. In late May, even before scrutiny about child separation had intensified, he tweeted: "Put pressure on the Democrats to end the horrible law that separates children from there [sic] parents once they cross the Border."

And as scrutiny intensified following my trip to Brownsville, he tweeted that "separating families at the Border is the fault of bad legislation passed by the Democrats."[6]

Wrong. There is no law requiring child separation.

One thing is for sure, both Donald and Melania Trump were paying attention to how child separation was registering with the public. Trump made his views known as always through his tweets. And Mrs. Trump scheduled a visit to the Upbring New Hope Children's Shelter in McAllen, Texas, on June 21. She met with the children and checked in with the staff about how they provide for the children. But what got the most attention was the coat she wore on the trip down to Texas: a coat emblazoned in large white letters on the back with the words I REALLY DON'T CARE. DO U?[7]

TWO

ZERO TOLERANCE

TRUMP'S STRATEGY OF SEPARATING CHILDREN FROM THEIR parents began long before Jeff Sessions announced the Zero Tolerance policy in May 2018.

On February 2, 2017, just 13 days after Trump's inauguration, John Lafferty—the Asylum Chief for the U.S. Citizenship and Immigration Services—briefed asylum officers on a new strategy. As reported by Reuters, DHS was developing a plan for separating women and children crossing into the United States "to deter mothers from migrating to the United States with their children."[1]

That statement has the two key elements that would appear time and time again: child separation and deterrence. The theory: If you hurt the families, particularly the children, it would discourage victims of war, famine, and persecution from seeking refuge in the United States. This theory is extremely questionable. When people are fleeing from extreme brutality and possible death, the prospect of some potential future action at a distant destination seems unlikely to deter them. But this we know for sure: Deliberately hurting children for any reason is a dark and evil policy.

The administration was, I believe, well aware of the impact child separation would have on children. If they weren't, all they had to do was to listen to Marielena Hincapié, Executive Director of the National Immigration Law Center. As she explained to Reuters in that initial report just weeks after Trump took office, the policy "could create lifelong psychological trauma, especially for children that have just completed a perilous journey from Central America."[2] Many child psychological experts have weighed in similarly.

To counter this concern, the administration worked from the beginning to develop the argument that their plan would actually help children. When Reuters asked DHS that March about their plan, DHS responded: "The journey north is a dangerous one with too many situations where children—brought by parents, relatives or smugglers—are often exploited, abused or may even lose their lives. With safety in mind, the Department of Homeland Security continually explores options that may discourage those from even beginning the journey."[3]

Later on, the administration would go even further, referring to the parents themselves as smugglers. This is quite a public relations spin. It is much more palatable for DHS to tell the American public that they are protecting children from smugglers than to concede that they are inflicting trauma by ripping children out of their parents' arms.

I'm guessing that someday we will find the document in which an enterprising communications consultant put forward this approach. It reminds me of when I was new in the Senate and stumbled across a memo by Frank Luntz, a Republican consultant. He said in that document that no matter what plan Democrats came up with for improving health care in America, the Republicans should call it a "government takeover."[4] I was outraged. I couldn't believe that he would recommend lying to the public with the result of making health care in America worse, inflicting pain and suffering on millions who needed better health care. I went to the Senate chamber, document in hand, to publicize and condemn the approach. It didn't work. Even though President Barack Obama adopted the Republican plan—an online marketplace where consumers could shop for insurance for plans from private companies like Kaiser and Blue Cross— the Republicans succeeded in selling the "government takeover" line to much of America. Luntz's 2009 deception became PolitiFact's 2010 Lie of the Year.[5] But it was too late.

* * *

The initial report on child separation was confirmed shortly afterward by John Kelly, then Secretary of Homeland Security and soon-to-be White House Chief of Staff. CNN's Wolf Blitzer asked Kelly if the report about plans to separate children from their parents was true. "Yes, I am considering—in order to deter more movement along this terribly dangerous network—I am considering exactly that," Kelly said.[6] He added that this would be good for the children: "We have tremendous experience in dealing with unaccompanied minors. We turn them over [to HHS] and they do a very, very good job of putting them in foster care or linking them up with parents or family members in the United States."[7]

In this statement, Kelly calls children separated from their parents "unaccompanied minors." They were clearly accompanied when they came to the border, but DHS labeled them "unaccompanied" after separating them from their parents. This made them indistinguishable from children who did come across the border by themselves. So when DHS transferred the children to HHS, HHS couldn't distinguish between the two groups, and didn't track the family connections for the children separated from their parents. This ended up making it very hard for the Trump administration to reunite the families when the court ordered it to do so.

Kelly's commentary also shows how little Kelly and the Trump team were thinking about the welfare of the children. They started working on this plan in the opening days of the administration. It would be 14 months later when Sessions went public and announced the official start of Zero Tolerance. And in those 14 months, the architects of this policy never developed a plan to keep track of the connection and location of the parents and their children. Was it incompetence? Or complete callousness? Maybe some of both.

Kelly reveals something else in that conversation with Wolf Blitzer: a complete determination to mislead the public about the fate of the children. He talks about sending the children to live with relatives or foster parents, in which case they would be sheltered in homes, enjoying playgrounds, and attending schools. He doesn't talk about the reality that they would first be sent to a system of child prisons, which would expand to hold 15,000 migrant child inmates by December 2018.

By April Kelly went further, framing child separation as an effective strategy against Transnational Criminal Organizations (TCOs). "Fewer people crossing the border illegally means...fewer people submitting themselves to the TCOs' dark and dangerous networks."[8]

Where I see desperate mothers, fathers, and children suffering pain inflicted by Trump's child separation policy, Trump and Kelly see an effective strategy against powerful criminal enterprises. Our views couldn't be more different.

Maybe the difference lies in how much weight you give to the pain and suffering you are causing others. Perhaps the difference in perspectives has roots in Trump's campaign. Candidate Trump had spent most of the presidential election demonizing and dehumanizing immigrants from Mexico and Central America by equating them to gang members, drug dealers, rapists, and murderers. Once elected President, Trump doubled down on the practice of degrading immigrants. In the same month that Sessions launched Zero Tolerance, Trump said about people coming into the U.S. or trying to come in: "These aren't people, these are animals." Later, Trump contended that he was only talking about gang members trying to come into the United States, but throughout his campaign and presidency he has broadly categorized immigrants from south of the border in intensely derogatory terms.[9]

If you dehumanize people, you can do awful things to them and somehow feel it is OK. You see this all the time. We can see it in foreign wars and conflicts around the world today, like the 2017 campaign of ethnic cleansing by the Buddhist Burmese government against the Muslim Rohingya ethnic group, which followed decades in which the government dehumanized the Rohingya.

And we can see it occur repeatedly in American history. The brutal decimation of Native Americans during colonization, when colonizers characterized natives as savages. The treatment of black Americans during slavery and Jim Crow, when white Americans found ways to categorize black Americans into less-deserving levels of humanity. And the degradation of the Japanese during World War Two and the Vietnamese in the 1960s and 1970s.

So possibly Trump's inner group of officials were infected by Trump's continuous drumbeat of remarks degrading immigrants, a drumbeat amplified in Trump's inner circle by the influence of Steve Bannon and Breitbart. The core group that turned Trump's campaign rhetoric about immigrants into reality were Sessions, Kelly, and two of Sessions' former senate aides: Stephen Miller, who was Sessions' former Communications Director, and Gene Hamilton, who became Senior Counselor to Kelly.

This group drove policy on immigration issues from the Muslim travel ban to ending the DACA protections for the Dreamers—undocumented immigrant children who came to our country as children and know no other land.

As the White House and the courts clashed over the Muslim travel ban and Trump prepared to cancel DACA, launching a public child separation campaign was one more way to wage war against immigrants.

* * *

After April 2017, Trump's child separation strategy disappeared from public view. The public comments from Kelly in March and April on child separation didn't catch the attention of most policy makers, including me. There were no congressional hearings on the issue because the leadership of the House and Senate, both held by Republicans, weren't about to look into anything that might embarrass the President. The news media quickly turned their attention to other scandals and challenges. And the Trump administration, having gotten an initial sense of public discomfort with the strategy, made sure not to publicize it.

Child separation went underground, but it didn't go away. A report of the Inspector General of HHS found that Attorney General Sessions had issued an internal memorandum in April 2017 prioritizing the prosecution of immigration offenses, and in July the El Paso sector of CBP implemented a child separation strategy.[10]

How many children were separated during this period beginning in early 2017 through the time Sessions launched Zero Tolerance in May 2018? Quite possibly thousands.

We will never know the exact number because the record keeping by the administration was atrocious. But the Inspector General concluded that "thousands of children may have been separated during an influx that began in 2017, before the accounting required by the Court." And the accounting required by the court added 2,737 more.

* * *

Why did the Trump team take child separation public in May 2018, after keeping it well hidden during the previous year? One explanation might be that a strategy based on deterrence doesn't work well if the strategy isn't publicized. Apprehensions had gone up at the southern border from about 20,000 in June 2017 to 50,000 in June 2018. Although that's a big increase, it was still way below the monthly peak of 200,000 hit in the year 2000.

There was another and potentially stronger reason for making the program public and expanding it exponentially: the midterm November elections. When Sessions announced Trump's Zero Tolerance policy, the elections were just six months away.

Immigration—or more precisely, generating fear of immigrants—has been a part of the Republican strategy of running on fear. To put it simply, Republicans run on fear and Democrats run on hope. Fear works for Republicans because they are the party more trusted by voters to keep our nation safe. Hope works for Democrats because they are the party more trusted to build a better future for families through investments in housing, health care, education, and jobs.

So each election season, the Republican strategists look for the things that they can publicize and amplify to scare the American public. In 2014, Ebola was going to kill us all. In 2016, ISIS and immigrants were going to kill us all. But what was going to work in November 2018? Ebola had broken out in the Democratic Republic of the Congo, but it just seemed too far away to be scary this time around. ISIS had lost almost all its territory. Urban crime has been way down, so that didn't seem like a strong candidate. The traditional topic of guns—especially the prospect of the government taking away your guns—would have been perfect, except for the fact that Republicans controlled every part of government.

What was left? Immigration.

It was time to crank up the immigrant fear machine in every way possible. So they did, and that included expanding child separation exponentially under the name of Zero Tolerance, while arguing publicly that it was all about stopping a wave of violent migrant predators from surging into America.

* * *

As the immigrant fear machine revved up, the truth was a victim.

The truth is that the number of undocumented immigrants caught at the border in 2017, Trump's first year in office, was the lowest number since 1971.[11] The truth is that the migrants arriving at the border have shifted from largely Mexican men seeking work to desperate families escaping violence in Central America. The truth is that migrants commit crimes in the United States at a lower rate than native-born Americans.[12] The truth is that during the first six years of the Obama administration, from 2009 to 2014, more Mexican nationals left the United States for Mexico than left Mexico for the United States.[13] The truth is that asylum is not automatically granted when requested. The burden of proof is on the asylum seeker and acquiring the documentation to establish one's case is difficult.[14]

The truth is that child separation will not work as a deterrent because as long as families face brutal violence and poverty, they will take their chances at the border. The truth is that there is no study or documentation that shows that child separation helps reduce crime in America. The truth is that there is plenty of evidence that the trauma from child separation causes enormous, long-lasting psychological damage to the children.

* * *

The Trump plan to amplify immigration before the 2018 election didn't just involve publicizing and amplifying child separation. On the second Monday in June, nine days after my first trip to McAllen and Brownsville, Jeff Sessions announced a ruling that made it extremely difficult for migrants to qualify for asylum based on the fear of domestic abuse or gang violence.[15]

His ruling involved determining which social groups merit special protection under our immigration system. Our law provides protection for groups that meet two criteria: The members of the group must share a characteristic that makes them particularly vulnerable to abuse; and the groups must come from a place or a nation where the government cannot or will not protect them. But because the immigration courts are under the Department of Justice of the executive branch, rather than our independent system of courts, the Attorney General can issue guidance on which groups meet these criteria.

When Sessions took office, the protected groups included LGBTQ individuals, relatives of dissidents, victim of gangs, and victims of domestic violence. Sessions' broad rule change—disqualifying victims of gangs and domestic violence—overturned a precedent set in the 2014 case of a Guatemalan woman, Aminta Cifuentes, who was severely abused by her husband for a decade, including acid burns and beatings late in her pregnancy.[16]

His ruling has a huge potential impact on migrants fleeing persecution in Central America because many of them are facing brutal violence from domestic partners or gangs. Gangs, in fact, are often the governing force in many communities in the region, operating with impunity while the government—corrupted by bribes from the gangs and drug cartels—looks the other way.

America is more connected to the violence in the Northern Triangle—the region comprising Guatemala, Honduras, and El Salvador—than many Americans realize. The gangs and drug cartels that have overwhelmed the governing institutions in the region are fortified by the cash and the guns that flow to the region from America. If they didn't have American dollars and weapons, the governments in those nations would have a much better chance of regaining control.

Groups that defend immigrants' rights saw Sessions' ruling as a huge step backward to a time when domestic violence was viewed as a private matter. Karen Musalo, a lawyer who leads the Center for Gender and Refugee Studies at the University of California, Hastings College of the Law, commented, "What this decision does is yank us all back to the Dark Ages of human rights and women's human rights and the conceptualization of it."[17]

Following Sessions' new rule in June, the number of asylum cases approved for migrants from Guatemala, El Salvador, and Honduras dropped roughly in half. Before the ruling, the number approved in 2018 was 20 to 30 percent. After the ruling, it was 10 to 15 percent.[18]

But did Sessions overstep his legal authority and violate underlying law? The ACLU filed suit in August 2018, contending that he did. They argued that "The new policies undermine the fundamental human rights of women, contradicting decades of settled domestic and international law recognizing gender-based persecution as a basis for asylum.

34

They also impermissibly undermine claims involving gang violence."[19]

By December 2018, a federal district court issued an injunction that restores the ability of migrants to pass the first hurdle in requesting asylum—the ability to proceed to an asylum hearing based on the assertion of credible fear of persecution or torture if you were to return to your own country—based on domestic violence or gang violence. This will undoubtedly be appealed. And it remains unclear how domestic and gang violence will be treated during final asylum hearings.

*　*　*

After I went down to McAllen and Brownsville in June and shined a spotlight on child separation, public outrage surged. A couple million people watched the Facebook Live video in which I attempted to gain access to the Casa Padre child prison in Brownsville. Other members of Congress started visiting and speaking up. Congresswoman Pramila Jayapal was one of the first, visiting a migrant caravan on the Mexican side of the border. Running for Senate in Texas, Congressman Beto O'Rourke protested a tent city for migrant children in Tornillo, Texas. Interest by media outlets was massive, including coverage of both child separation and the system of child prisons and family internment camps.

But perhaps most powerfully, church leaders voiced outrage. More than 300 Catholic bishops from across the country condemned both child separation and Sessions' new rule on protected social groups at their spring assembly in Fort Lauderdale, Florida. "These vulnerable women will now face return to the extreme dangers of domestic violence in their home country," said Msgr. J. Brian Bransfield on behalf of Cardinal Daniel DiNardo. "This decision negates decades of precedence that have provided protection to women fleeing domestic violence." The bishops said clearly that the separation of families needed to stop. "Our government has the discretion in our laws to ensure that young children are not separated from their parents and exposed to irreparable harm and trauma," said Bransfield. "Families are the foundational element of our society and they must be able to stay together. Separating babies from their mothers is not the answer and is immoral."[20]

Outraged condemnation of child separation came from across the religious spectrum, including some conservative evangelical leaders who are normally rock-ribbed in their defense of Trump. Rev. Franklin Graham told the Christian Broadcasting Network, "I think it's disgraceful. It's terrible to see families ripped apart and I don't support that one bit."[21] At the same time, the Southern Baptist Convention passed a resolution calling for immigration reform that maintained "the priority of family unity" and declaring that "any form of nativism, mistreatment, or exploitation is inconsistent with the gospel of Jesus Christ."[22]

Sessions pushed back against the religious leaders by citing the Bible. "Let me take an aside to discuss concerns raised by our church friends about separating families," he told a friendly group of law-enforcement officers in Fort Wayne, Indiana. "Many of the criticisms raised in recent days are not fair or logical and some are contrary to law. First, illegal entry into the United States is a crime—as it should be. Persons who violate the law of our nation are subject to prosecution. I would cite you to the Apostle Paul and his clear and wise command in Romans 13, to obey the laws of the government because God has ordained them for the purpose of order."[23]

I have my own suggestion of Bible verses that Sessions might want to contemplate. For wisdom from the Old Testament, how about this from Psalm 82: "Defend the poor and fatherless: do justice to the afflicted and needy. Deliver the poor and needy: rid them out of the hand of the wicked."

For wisdom from the New Testament, consider Jesus' parable of the Good Samaritan in the book of Luke. Jesus tells the story of a traveler left half-dead and beaten by robbers on the road to Jericho. Three men pass by, but only the third, the Samaritan, crosses the road to assist the man. He uses this story to explain what it means to "Love your neighbor as yourself" and says to the expert in the law: "Go and do likewise."

After quoting the Bible, Sessions went on to argue that that the U.S. "goes to extraordinary lengths to protect them [the children] while the parents go through a short detention period. Please note, Church friends, that if the adults go to one of our many ports of entry to claim asylum, they are not prosecuted and the family stays intact pending the legal process."[24]

A short detention? I don't know how long "a short detention" is in Sessions' mind, but I think most people would assume that he was talking about hours or days. This is not the case. The time of separation can be months or even years. The Inspector General of Homeland Security observed that at the CBP processing centers, the CBP "held alien children separated from their parents for extended periods in facilities intended solely for short-term detention."[25] And after the processing center, migrant children are often held for weeks or months in the migrant child prison gulag before being placed with a sponsor.

And much longer periods of separation can occur when the U.S. government has deported the parent while the child remains in the United States. "Permanent separation. It happens," said John Sandweg, who was Acting Director of ICE in 2014. "You could easily end up in a situation where the gap between a parent's deportation and a child's deportation is years." In that case, it could be hard or even impossible for the family to reunite, and the children will eventually be adopted.[26]

Families can claim asylum at ports of entry? Sessions' "ports of entry" claim is one of the really big lies told by the Trump administration. On various occasions the administration has condemned "illegal entry" into the United States between ports of entry and suggested that everything will be just fine if migrants seeking asylum instead go to the "legal" ports of entry.

The truth is that the Trump administration has been systematically blocking migrants from seeking asylum at ports of entry, driving them back into the hands of gangs in Mexico. I heard about this on my first trip to McAllen, when Jennifer Harbury told us about the migrants camped on the Reynosa bridge. And I saw it with my own eyes on my second trip on Father's Day two weeks later, when the CBP had three or four officers on the same bridge blocking migrants from crossing and asserting asylum. Shutting down the port of entry to asylum seekers and leaving them stranded in dangerous territory in Mexico gives them a powerful incentive to travel parallel to the border to find a spot where they can cross into the United States between ports of entry—the exact behavior Trump tells the public he is trying to stop.

* * *

After my trips in June, the horrors of child separation were so clear to me that I thought I might be able to help Jeff Sessions understand that this was a terrible policy. I felt I had some personal foundation for an honest conversation with him. We had served in the Senate together. And three years earlier we had worked together on a retirement plan for individual savings that would automatically put 3 percent of your income in a broad, diversified stock portfolio unless you opted out. It would be a powerful complement to Social Security.

I had met with Sessions several times to brainstorm about it and develop the possibility we would introduce it together.

I love to put forward bills on a bipartisan basis; it greatly increases the chance that the idea will gain momentum and win passage. Sessions told me several times that he liked the plan, and believed it would be great for working families, and that he was almost ready to partner on it. But I could never get him to ink the deal. Despite that failure and despite our vast differences on many topics, I still felt like we had a working relationship and that a personal conversation might help bridge the enormously different perspectives we had on child separation. I thought he needed to hear from someone outside the administration who had seen child separation in action.

I called him up, Jeff to Jeff. I explained that I had been looking into the effects of child separation and would like to share some thoughts with him. "The policy on the border is really hurting kids," I began. I went on to explain the pain experienced by the children and the parents. "This policy is hurting people in a way that's just so out of character for America. This isn't a good way to discourage refugees from coming to our border. The world isn't going to smile on this."

"Oh no, no, no, Jeff," he replied. "I'm protecting the kids."

"How are you protecting the kids?" I asked, thinking about all those kids I'd seen at the McAllen processing center and the former Walmart in Brownsville.

"Well, we're helping kids by deterring them from coming. We're preventing them from suffering the challenges of the journey," he argued. This turns out to be almost exactly what DHS told Julia Edwards Ainsley, an enterprising reporter for

Reuters, when she asked DHS about plans to separate children from their parents more than a year earlier, in March 2017.[27] Sessions was really good at sticking to the prescribed talking points.

"Jeff," I pressed, "these are families that are fleeing persecution and horrific circumstances, whether it's from drug gangs or any other form of oppression. They are going to keep coming. Inflicting trauma on them when they arrive at the border just isn't the way to treat people. You've got to put an end to this. This is just not unfolding the way you think it is. Step back and see the bigger picture."

Sessions was unmoved. "We make life better for them because they will not undertake that hard journey," he said. "It will spare the children if they only listen to us."

"Jeff, the American people are not going to view treating these kids like this as something beneficial for migrant children," I replied. "Because it's not."

* * *

A deeply troubling aspect of the debate over child separation is that the officials of the Trump administration lie so easily and so often. I'm not used to saying someone lies. I'd rather say that they bend the truth. Or tell less than the full story. But lives are at stake. And you can't trust anything you are told. The CBP officer at the McAllen processing center said the system for tracking parents and children worked perfectly. That was completely wrong. When Sessions told the public that if migrants just came to the ports of entry,

they could ask for asylum and all would be great, he knew—
and now all of us know—that our CBP has been blocking
migrants from asking for asylum at the ports of entry.

Trump lies about so many aspects of immigration it is hard
to know where to begin, but perhaps the most damaging
lie is that the migrants are a horde of murderers and rapists
surging into America, when in fact they are men looking for
work and families fleeing violence; and they commit fewer
crimes than native-born Americans.

Still, I was unprepared for the level of DHS Secretary
Kirstjen Nielsen's deceptions. Just a few days before Christmas 2018, she appeared in front of the House Judiciary Committee to discuss the Trump administration's immigration
policies. As head of the department that had helped develop
and implement family separation, she testified that "we've
never had a policy for family separation." She stated that
there was a database and "we know where all the children
were, we knew where all the parents were," when CBP—
which is part of DHS—had completely failed to track the
connections between the children and their parents.[28]

When a reporter asked if the administration was using
child separation to send a message for migrants seeking
asylum to stay out, she said, "I find that offensive." She
responded that way even though John Kelly, her predecessor
and then Trump's Chief of Staff, had reiterated on NPR the
month before that "a big name of the game is deterrence."[29]
And she claimed her department was watching out for the
health of migrant children by encouraging them "to go to a

port of entry," even as her department's officers were blocking children from setting foot on American soil at ports of entry, leaving them stranded at great risk in Mexican border towns.

Child separation didn't happen due to the random actions of rogue agents. It happened because of deliberate action by Trump's administration. Asylum Chief John Lafferty briefed his officers on it in the first two weeks of Trump taking office. John Kelly, then Trump's Secretary of DHS, discussed it with the press the following month. A pilot project was initiated shortly thereafter. A December 2017 document I publicly disclosed from Kirstjen Nielsen's office showed extensive planning for a broader program of "separating family units, placing the adults in adult detention, and placing the minors under the age of 18 in the custody of HHS as unaccompanied alien children."[30] That memo didn't write itself. But despite all of that, she couldn't honestly discuss the strategy with Congress.

Lying to Congress is a crime that corrodes public trust and our American principles of good government. Since Nielsen was under oath when she lied to Congress, I wrote to the FBI Director Christopher Wray urging him to immediately investigate whether Nielsen's testimony constituted perjury and false statements to Congress. The FBI, of course, is part of the Department of Justice operating previously under Sessions and now under Bill Barr. As far as we know, the FBI has taken no action.

In June 2018 public pressure and a court decision would

end Trump's child separation policy. No longer could CBP tear children out of their parents' arms. But despite this official end, some child separations continued. In March 2019, the administration reported to a federal judge that they had removed an additional 245 children from their families. The reasons were often for minor violations that would normally not lead to losing custody of a child, like a drunk-driving conviction or possession of a small amount of marijuana. The children ranged from newborn babies to older teenagers, and some parents were deported while their children remained in the United States. And because records were often inaccurate or nonexistent, the number of separated children could be much higher.[31]

THREE

ZERO HUMANITY

TRUMP NAMED HIS POLICY OF CHILD SEPARATION ZERO TOL-
erance, but a more accurate name might well be Zero
Humanity.

When I talked directly to Jeff Sessions about this policy,
he never deviated from the argument he was protecting children. He was disciplined in his message. He had the same
message for me that he had for the public: The United States
"goes to extraordinary lengths to protect" the children. We
heard this same message from Secretary Nielsen. We even
heard it from DHS Secretary John Kelly in March 2017: The
children "will be well cared for as we deal with their parents," and HHS does "a very, very good job of putting them
in foster care."

The administration officials are generally right if you
equate good care with a clean mattress and three meals a
day. But they are wrong, profoundly wrong, if you are talking about medical care at the border or the psychological

wounds to children and parents from detention and child separation.

In December 2018, Jakelin Caal Maquin, a seven-year-old Guatemalan girl, died under American care.

Jakelin and her father, Nery Caal, come from an impoverished region in rural Guatemala. They were poor. The family of seven survived on $5 a day. Jakelin had never owned a toy or a pair of shoes. Jakelin's grandfather remembers her jumping for joy when she found out about the trip. They hoped to make it to America and send funds back to the family. Instead, Jakelin died.

Jakelin and her father crossed a remote section of the U.S.-Mexico border on the evening of December 6 as part of a group of 162 people. They turned themselves in to the Border Patrol and were held at Camp Bounds, which has limited staff and facilities. Her father raised concerns about Jakelin's health while there, but the Border Patrol determined that the fastest way to get help was to bus her to Lordsburg ninety miles away. At some point near the end of the bus ride, Jakelin stopped breathing. She was revived by an EMT. A helicopter took her to a hospital in El Paso, where she died shortly after midnight.

Immigration advocates blamed DHS for her death, and DHS blamed her father. Here is what we can conclude: The journey is inherently dangerous. Migrants often cross the desert with insufficient food and water. Dehydration is a life-threatening risk. It is estimated that hundreds of migrants die crossing the desert each year. But knowing this, it makes sense for Border Patrol officers to be equipped to check on the health of migrants when they are picked up. Officers should be able to give a basic health check to children in the field or immediately upon arriving at a Border Patrol facility, and be prepared with plans for getting a sick child to a hospital quickly.

Furthermore, one reason migrants seek to cross at remote border points is that the CBP is blocking them from requesting asylum at ports of entry. In so doing, CBP is contributing to the circumstances in which children have longer, more difficult journeys that involve greater health risks. This needs to change.

Scott Allen and Pamela McPherson were health inspectors in the migrant detention system for four years. They wrote in the *Washington Post* that "the news that Jakelin had died in U.S. Customs and Border Protection custody after crossing the border from Mexico during her journey from Guatemala came as a shock to many, but not to us...We fear that unless U.S. authorities stop detaining children, Jakelin will not be the last child to die in government custody."[1]

She wasn't. On Christmas Eve, five days after the *Washington Post* published Scott and Pamela's article, Felipe Gómez Alonzo died in U.S. custody. He was eight years old.

Felipe Gómez Alonzo lived in a shack with a tin roof, dirt floors, and no electricity in the remote Guatemalan village of Yalambojoch, which had a population of 1,000. Six members of the family shared a bedroom. In this village of deep poverty, there are a few modern two-story homes sporting tile roofs, thanks to remittances from abroad. The village is nine hours from Guatemala's capital on a route that includes a dangerous dirt track winding through the mountains. The residents speak Chuj, an indigenous Mayan language, and most spent years displaced from their village during Guatemala's thirty-six-year civil war, which at times included the military going village to village massacring residents.

Peace enabled villagers to return to Yalambojoch, but the end of the war did not change the extortion and corruption that continue to drain rural resources and accentuate massive income and wealth inequality in an economy controlled by a small class of urban power brokers. As reported in *The Guardian*, "migration has long been seen [as] a reasonable response to the country's hardship, racism and violence."[2]

Felipe's mother, Catarina Alonzo, said that the family hoped the father, Gómez Pérez, would be able to find work, pay off their debts, and send money back to the family. He only earned about $6 per day in the village. Alonzo said her son was happy to journey with his father and had hoped to study and have a bicycle of his own.

Felipe and his father crossed the Rio Grande and presented themselves to the Border Patrol on December 18. They were held at the Paso Del Norte processing center for two days, and then another two days at the El Paso Border Patrol station, before being sent to the Alamogordo Border Patrol station eighty miles away.

At Alamogordo, Felipe's health deteriorated. He was sent to Gerald Champion Regional Medical Center nearby with possible influenza symptoms. He was diagnosed with a common cold and given Tylenol. His fever spiked to 103 degrees. The medical team prescribed an antibiotic, and he was released to a temporary holding facility at the Highway 70 checkpoint. Agents gave him the prescribed antibiotic that evening. He started vomiting at 7 p.m. Three hours later agents took him back to Gerald Champion Regional Medical Center. He lost consciousness on the trip back and died shortly thereafter.

I joined the House Hispanic Caucus on a trip to Texas and New Mexico to learn more about these deaths and the treatment of migrant children. Congressman Joaquin Castro of Texas led the group. Congresswomen Veronica Escobar and Xochitl Torres Small hosted us. Escobar represents El Paso, Texas, and Torres Small represents Alamogordo, New Mexico. Other participants included Jerry Nadler (NY), David Cicilline (RI), and three members from California: Grace Napolitano, Nanette Barragan, and Salud Carbajal.

In El Paso, Escobar took me to look at the very place where Felipe and his dad had crossed the Rio Grande. The fence is high there, but the Border Patrol officers had left the gate open after driving a utility vehicle into the no-man's-land between the fence and the Rio Grande. I walked through the gate to inspect more closely where Felipe and his dad had been. I imagined them coming across that patch of ground, hearts beating fast, knowing that this was a perilous phase of their journey. They were probably praying that they could quickly get the attention of Border Patrol officers so

49

they could surrender before they were snatched by one of the Mexican gangs that control portions of the border and insist on getting paid before they will allow a migrant to cross into America.

The entire delegation then traveled up to the Alamogordo CBP station to learn more. We looked at the *hieleras* where Felipe and his dad were held. We asked the officers there a lot of questions about the care of the migrants and particularly of the children. And one thing I kept hearing was that the officers had conducted multiple "wellness checks" on the migrants. These same "wellness" or "welfare" checks show up in the point-by-point record of Felipe's journey released by ICE. El Paso Border Patrol Station: seventeen checks. Alamogordo Station: "several" checks. Highway 70 temporary holding facility: "several" checks.

I asked what a wellness check consisted of. "An officer passes by the holding cell and asks if anyone needs assistance" was the answer. That blew me away. When I had heard the term "wellness check" or "welfare check," I pictured a direct medical inspection from a qualified individual who did things like checking the child's eyes and ears and throat, asking when he or she had last had water and food, inquiring about pains or health troubles, and taking the child's temperature and blood pressure.

But no. A wellness check simply meant asking a crowd of migrants filling the *hieleras* if anyone needed help. And when migrants in a cell are asked if they need any assistance, they are reluctant to speak up out of fear that they will be separated from their friends and family or otherwise be sin-gled out for unpleasant treatment. So this type of wellness check is often useless in identifying health problems.

The CBP officers at Alamogordo said they were working to improve the health screenings for migrants at the bor-der stations and processing centers. They introduced us to Dr. Alexander Eastman, who DHS had hired to develop an improved strategy for checking on the health status of migrant children.

A third child died in U.S. custody after entering the coun-try as an unaccompanied minor in April. The 16-year-old Guatemalan boy fell ill while living in a Texas shelter for migrant children. He was sent to a hospital and treated before being released the same day. The next day, he was sent back to the hospital where he spent several days in intensive care. Officials refused to say how long he had been in the country or where his parents were.[3]

* * *

For every migrant child who dies, thousands suffer signifi-cant trauma. Experts tell us that children are resilient, and that many will recover to have happy and productive lives. But many others will carry psychological wounds that will challenge them for their lifetimes. Why would we do this to children? It is wrong and evil.

Hearing administration officials say how wonderfully they are caring for migrant children is disturbing and infu-riating. Disturbing because they don't recognize or won't acknowledge the damage done to children. Enraging because we have not been able to put an end to it. It is like listening to someone who kidnapped a child then defend his crime to the world by saying what good care—great food and a really clean mattress—he provided. Providing good food and a clean mattress doesn't negate the horrific trauma of kidnapping a child, and it doesn't negate the horrific trauma of child separation. Moreover, the United States often hasn't provided great care.

The warnings from medical experts came time and time again. In May 2017, a full year before Sessions announced the Zero Tolerance policy, the American Academy of Pediatrics issued a detailed report that expressed multiple concerns about the medical treatment of migrant children.

Their concerns included the CBP's "limited medical screening" when they processed the children. They did not conduct complete medical histories or physical examinations, including the children's vital signs. The Academy also had concerns about the migrant child prisons: "Visits to family detention centers in 2015 and 2016 by pediatric and mental health advocates revealed discrepancies between the standards outlined by ICE and the actual services provided, including inadequate or inappropriate immunizations, delayed medical care, inadequate education services, and limited mental health services." They concluded, "The Department of Homeland Security facilities do not meet the basic standards for the care of children in residential settings."[4]

A year later, in September 2018, a team of medical experts

from Stanford University went to check on the health of migrant children detained in America's migrant child prisons. They were allowed to visit the children because the Flores Settlement—an agreement settling a legal challenge to child imprisonment in 1997—set down the treatment and conditions required for children's care and provided for inspections to see if these conditions were being met.

One of the medical experts summarized his observations: "One major concern was that the infrastructure of health care for children and their families coming through the asylum process is woefully inadequate in the border communities. The frontline health providers who work in the border area clinics are often overwhelmed by the challenge. In some measure, they have to rely on volunteers coming from around the United States. Providers will come in with good intentions, but their very short-term contributions are no substitute for a high-quality clinical infrastructure. A caring volunteer neurosurgeon may help fill in, but when is the last time that this doc saw a 5-year-old with diarrhea and PTSD?"[5]

The impact on mental health of imprisoning children is probably much greater than on physical health. The psychological scars from child separation come in many forms. Ana Fernandes was separated from her son Thiago, age five, for fifty days. She says he isn't the same boy. After reunification, he pled to be breast-fed although she hasn't nursed in years. He hid behind the sofa. He didn't want to talk to anyone.[6]

These stories abound. In many cases, the children, having been abandoned once, fear abandonment again. Others carry enormous anger with their parents. Others, having been duped by a border official who separated them from their parents with a bogus invitation to have a meal or to play with other children, have great difficulty trusting what they are told. Having been lied to by one figure of authority, how do you trust the next?

The American Academy of Pediatrics' report found that young detainees in the United States showed "high rates of post-traumatic stress disorder, anxiety, depression, suicidal ideation, and other behavioral problems." ICE's own advisory committee on family detention centers found that "detention is generally neither appropriate nor necessary for families—and that detention or the separation of families for purposes of immigration enforcement or management are never in the best interest of children."[7]

Other experts continue to weigh in. Philip G. Schrag, an expert on asylum and a professor of law at Georgetown University, drew attention to the psychological damage caused by child separation: "I think it's absolutely wrenching psychologically and terrible for both the children and the parents," he said. "What are we doing to those children psychologically that will haunt us years down the road if they become Americans?"[8] Of course, those same psychological problems will haunt them whether they gain legal status, or are deported.

Children thrive when they feel safe and secure. But regaining that sense of security can be very difficult. Joanna Franchini works with Together & Free, which coordinates volunteers who work with migrant children across the nation. She observes that "our volunteers are seeing the significant and real toll that these traumatic separations have had on these children's and these families' lives, which persist even after reunification."[9] Psychology Professor Johanna Bick, an expert on childhood trauma, notes that "there is no greater threat to a child's emotional well-being than being separated from a primary caregiver. Even if it was for a short period, for a child, that's an eternity . . . The bad news is that the first few years of life are a sensitive period of brain development; what happens can have dramatic impact later."[10]

* * *

And have no doubt, the parents suffer as well as children. This was abundantly clear when I led a congressional delegation to visit a group of mothers separated from their children and imprisoned at Port Isabel, an ICE prison for women outside Brownsville.

We met around a dozen migrant women dressed in dark blue-and-red prison uniforms in a communal room that also served as a chapel. I moved the benches in the room into a circle so we could talk to each other more easily. The women began telling their stories, and they started to cry. They talked about the violence that had driven them to the border, and they talked about the pain they suffered being forced apart from their children.

"They took my child," one of the women shared, "but nobody ever once asked me if he had any medical needs. He doesn't speak English and doesn't know his own medical needs. He needs insulin and other medicines. I have no idea if he was seen by a doctor or if he will survive."

It seemed so obvious and yet we were so clueless: Younger children may be completely ignorant of, or unable to recount, their own medical conditions and the drugs or treatment they need.

One mother described the complete confusion of her situation. "I have no idea where my son is," she said. "This is a big country and I think he might be in New York. But I don't know where that is in relation to where we are."

Another mother described how she thought the only hope for her daughter was to arrange for her sister to adopt her. She explained that she had been told that she had two choices: deportation or indefinite detention. She believed that it would be catastrophic for her daughter's welfare if her daughter was deported. But she also knew that it would be catastrophic for her daughter to be without a mother. Her solution: Arrange for her sister to be her daughter's new mother.

The fathers feel the pain, too. I heard the anxiety and desperation in their stories when I met with fathers separated from their children at the prison in Sheridan, Oregon.

But the story that sticks in my mind the most is of Marco Antonio Muñoz, a father from Honduras. I never met him and I never will, because he is dead. His might have been the first death stemming from Trump's and Sessions' Zero Tolerance policy. Sessions officially announced large-scale child separation on May 7, 2018. Four days later, Border Patrol officers apprehended Muñoz, his wife, and their three-year-old son as they crossed the Rio Grande near Granjeno, Texas. They were taken to the Rio Grande Valley Central Processing Center.

At the processing center, Muñoz and his family asked for asylum. It is not clear how this request was treated. What is clear is that Border Patrol agents told the family they would be separated. Muñoz was greatly agitated by learning that his family would be split up. The following day, May 12, they moved him to a jail in Starr County, Texas, about forty miles away. A CBP spokesman explained that they moved him because he "became disruptive and combative." A report posted by the Texas Attorney General described him as "combative and noncompliant," causing officers to place him in a padded cell that night.[11] By morning, he was dead. In the report, his death is described as suicide by self-strangulation and hanging.

Justin Tullius, an attorney with a Texan nonprofit organization that assists refugees, observed that both detention and child separation put enormous stress on adults: "We've worked with parents who have shared suicidal thoughts and who have attempted to take their own lives because of the experience of detention," Tullius said. "We can't allow policies that traumatize parents and children. Families must be allowed to go through the process of seeking protection in the U.S. together, without unnecessary and harmful separation."[12]

* * *

As I visited the various facilities in the immigration system, it was hard to escape the sense that beyond the migrant children and migrant parents, child separation is creating a third set of victims, the officers and officials of agencies that implement the policies: Border Patrol, CBP, ORR, and ICE, along with the policy makers at HHS, DOJ, and DHS who have a role in designing or implementing the child separation policy.

I think back to the first group of CBP officials I met at the McAllen border processing center. I asked them how they felt about implementing the new child separation policy. After a silence, one official responded: "We don't make the policies. It's our job to implement them." They didn't seem very happy about it.

What would it feel like to take a screaming child out of a parent's arms? Or a sullen child away from a screaming parent? Or to lie to a mother when you took her child, saying that you were taking the child for a medical check, when you knew that parent would soon be crying out and asking where her child was? What would it be like to work at Port Isabel prison, and hear migrant mothers sobbing as they worried about their children? Or to work at a migrant prison full of separated girls like Yaquelin Contreras, some of whom thought they might never see their mothers again and others who concluded that their parents had abandoned them? The darkness, the evil, of child separation damages the souls of everyone it touches.

Zero Tolerance is Zero Humanity.

FOUR

REUNIFICATION

YAQUELIN CONTRERAS AND HER MOTHER, ALBERTINA, MY guests at Trump's 2019 State of the Union speech, were living testimony to reunification. The impact of public opinion and a court challenge had brought an official end to one phase of Trump's child separation policy.

Yaquelin was taken from her mother soon after they crossed into America. For two months they were in the same state, but far apart. Albertina was locked up in El Paso, in the most western arm of Texas. Yaquelin was more than 800 miles away at Southwest Key's Casa Antigua facility in San Benito, a small town just miles from the Gulf Coast.

Tuesday, June 26, 2018, was a big day in Albertina's journey. On that day Judge Dana Sabraw of the U.S. District Court in San Diego issued a sweeping injunction that put an immediate end to most family separations at the border and ordered expedited reunification of separated families. The response was swift. ICE released Albertina from incarceration on the very same day. The officials gathered the parents, informed them of their impending release, and explained that they were going to meet their kids. You can imagine the soaring emotions of the parents like Albertina after months of imprisonment and separation from their children.

But this ended up being one more cruel twist in the treatment of the mothers and fathers. ICE put Albertina and other parents on a bus and drove them a short distance to a local charity that was operating a respite center. Albertina was on one of the first buses that rolled up to the two-story redbrick Annunciation House in El Paso. She got out and searched for Yaquelin, but her daughter was nowhere to be found. It was up to the staff at Annunciation House to explain that the children weren't there, and that they, the staff, had no idea where the children were.

The volunteers at Annunciation House did all they could to assist Albertina and the other parents. They put Albertina in contact with her relatives in Murfreesboro, Tennessee, a town thirty-four miles southeast of Nashville. They were also able to arrange a flight to Nashville with a donated air ticket. Taylor Levy, the Legal Coordinator at Annunciation House, called her friend Andrew Free, an attorney in Nashville, and he agreed to provide pro bono legal services.

Now Albertina had a home base from which she could work toward connecting and reunifying with her daughter.

ORR wouldn't release Yaquelin to her care without first getting the fingerprints of everyone in her household. While the argument for fingerprints is to protect children from predators, the Trump administration was giving those fingerprints to ICE, which was using them to identify and deport migrants. In Albertina's case, it seemed totally unjustified since ORR was releasing Yaquelin to her mother, not some distant relative or unidentified stranger. Albertina's legal team made that point in court and won Yaquelin's release.

ORR put Yaquelin onto a plane, and on July 12 Albertina went to the Nashville airport to reunite with her daughter. This time, she wasn't disappointed. A group of Nashville well-wishers went with her, and they gave Yaquelin a celebratory welcome, including flowers, a plush toy rabbit, a song, and a bag of peanut butter cups.

Six months after this reunion, Albertina and Yaquelin joined me in the Capitol for Trump's State of the Union speech. They attended to help publicize the tragedy of child separation and the plight of children locked up in migrant child prisons. I walked them up to their balcony seats in the House of Representatives, where they sat and listened to a speech by the very same man who had ordered the child separation policy that brought so much pain to them and so many others.

True to form, Trump spent a good portion of his State of the Union fearmongering about immigrants. He equated immigrants to gang members. He talked about countless

Americans murdered by immigrants. He talked about how the criminals will keep "streaming" in without a wall. He didn't remind us that we are a nation made up substantially of immigrants and their descendants. He didn't discuss Lady Liberty holding up a lamp to the homeless and tempest tossed. He didn't talk about the enormous contributions of immigrants to our culture and our economy. He didn't remind us that immigrants commit fewer crimes per capita than native-born Americans.

I wish he had taken a moment in his speech to look up and see Albertina and Yaquelin, acknowledge the trials they have endured, and guarantee that they and all migrants will be treated with respect and dignity as they await their asylum hearings. A different President might have told them that if they win asylum, he wishes them all the best and knows that they will make great contributions to their adopted community and country. That would have been a wonderful birthday present for Yaquelin, who was celebrating her twelfth birthday that very day.

* * *

Judge Sabraw's injunction ending child separation and ordering family reunifications was in response to a case the ACLU had filed on behalf of a Congolese mother who was separated from her seven-year-old daughter in 2017, and then broadened to include other families in similar situations. They were kept together for five days after requesting asylum. Then, according to the lawsuit filed in federal court, the immigration officials took the child away "screaming and crying, pleading with guards not to take her away from her mother."[1]

Sabraw ordered federal officials to do four things: stop detaining parents away from their minor children; enable all children to talk to their parents within ten days; reunify parents with their minor children under age five within 14 days; and reunify parents with minor children aged between five and seventeen years within thirty days. In issuing the order, Judge Sabraw was fiercely critical of the Trump administration: "The unfortunate reality is that under the present system migrant children are not accounted for with the same efficiency and accuracy as property," he wrote.[2]

He described a chaotic situation that the administration had created and was unable to solve due to its incompetence: "The practice of separating these families was implemented without any effective system or procedure for (1) tracking the children after they were separated from their parents, (2) enabling communication between the parents and their children after separation, and (3) reuniting the parents and children after the parents are returned to immigration custody following completion of their criminal sentence. This is a startling reality."

One doesn't have to think long about some of the fundamental measures the Trump administration could have prepared and used to address such issues. Make sure that the various immigration databases talk to each other. Make sure, at least, that each database records the family connections before separating families. Use photos, fingerprints, and DNA samples to help track connections. Give each immigrant a bracelet with file numbers for locating all their family members in the immigration databases. Give each immigrant a wallet card, in their own language, on how to use free phones or free phone numbers at immigration facilities for connecting with family members. And so forth.

The deadline for reuniting migrant children under age five with their parents was Tuesday, July 10. Of the 102 children HHS identified in that category, only 75 qualified for reunification because of factors that made the parents of the rest ineligible for reunification, such as an existing criminal record. Because the information connecting children and parents was so convoluted, the reunifications went slowly. On July 10, the deadline for children under five, reunifications for only four of the seventy-five eligible children had been confirmed.[3]

When the thirty day deadline for reuniting all children arrived on Thursday, July 26, the administration was still scrambling. HHS Secretary Alex Azar had testified to the Senate Finance Committee in June that "I could at the stroke of keystrokes ... within seconds, could find any child within our care for any parent."[4] By the end of July, the whole world knew that his assertion was pure fiction.

On the thirty-day deadline, Judge Sabraw expressed his dismay and anger over this colossal incompetence. Referring to CBP, ORR and ICE, he fumed that "there were three agencies, and each was like its own stovepipe. Each had its own boss, and they did not communicate. What was lost in the process was the family. The parents didn't know where the children were, and the children didn't know where the parents were. And the government didn't know, either."[5]

*   *   *

Family connections weren't the only thing the administration couldn't keep track of. They also hadn't kept track of the location of the children who had been released to sponsors from the migrant child prisons. That led to *New York Times* headlines like this in September 2018: "U.S. Loses Track of Another 1,500 Migrant Children, Investigators Find."[6] Not only had the administration lost track of those 1,500 children in the first six months of 2018, they had lost track of an additional 1,475 children in 2017, according to a report by Steven Wagner, Acting Assistant Secretary of the Administration for Children and Families at HHS.[7] Quite simply, the administration has been doing a terrible job of staying in touch with migrant adults and children as they await their asylum hearings.

Both Republicans and Democrats were outraged. Senator Rob Portman (a Republican from Ohio) and Senator Dick Blumenthal (a Democrat from Connecticut) introduced a bill to address this. Portman observed that the act "will ensure that we keep track of unaccompanied minors in our country, which will both help protect them from trafficking and abuse as well as help ensure they appear for their immigration court proceedings."[8] The Trump administration had defended child separation as a remedy for human trafficking, and then exposed children to the risk of trafficking by failing to keep in contact with the children and their sponsors.

Another factor making reunifying families complicated was that the administration had deported many of the parents. HHS Secretary Alex Azar blamed the parents for that separation: "We often do find, when a parent is deported, that they ask the child to remain separate and remain in this country," he explained.[9]

This is far from the full story. As detailed in various court filings, the administration used many tricks to deport the parents. They were asked to sign forms written in English that they did not understand that relinquished their rights to be reunited with their children. They were told that deportation was the fastest way to be reunited with their children. They were told that applying for asylum would take many months and that they would not be able to see their children for that time period. They were given incomplete information on their options, including the possibility of seeking to live with their children and a sponsor while pursuing asylum.

Trump didn't want to take responsibility for reuniting the families with deported parents. On August 2, 2018, the Justice Department filed a court document arguing that immigration advocacy groups, particularly the ACLU, should shoulder the responsibility for finding the 500 parents the administration had deported without their children. Judge

Sabraw admonished the administration for trying to foist this responsibility on to anyone else: "The reality is that for every parent who is not located, there will be a permanent orphaned child, and that is 100% the responsibility of the administration."[10]

The hostility of the administration to its responsibility to reunite families arises again and again. In March 2019, a group of deported parents returned to the southern border seeking reunification with their sons and daughters held in the U.S. A few have been able to reconnect with their children, but ICE locked up seventeen of the parents with no indication of when they would be set free. Jose Eduardo, who has been separated from his daughter Yaimy for ten months, said that the last time he saw her "she was standing in a frigid border patrol holding cell." After he returned from immigration court, Yaimy was missing. "Where is my daughter?" he demanded. They refused to provide information, saying inaccurately: "We don't know."[11]

I joined a group of Democratic senators led by Senator Catherine Cortez Masto to demand answers from DHS Secretary Kirstjen Nielsen: "These parents have again been separated from the children they presented themselves with, further compounding the fear, harm, and trauma they have already experienced. It is imperative that these parents be released, reunited with their children, and allowed to continue their cases in immigration court."[12]

The Trump administration has also moved slowly on reuniting children they separated from parents before

Sessions announced the official policy in May 2018. The challenge is that the government has to review 47,000 immigration files of children it labeled "unaccompanied" in its computer database to figure out which ones were actually accompanied by parents. The administration asked the court for two additional years to go through their files. The ACLU swiftly responded, "The administration refuses to treat the family separation crisis it created with urgency. The government swiftly gathered resources to tear families apart. It must do the same to fix the damage."[13]

I couldn't agree more.

FIVE

INTERNMENT CAMPS

TRUMP HAD WHAT HE THOUGHT WAS AN EXCELLENT PLAN to respond to the public outrage over child separations: family internment camps. The strategy was to end child separation through the long-term lockup of refugee children and parents together in a vast system of family prisons. On June 20, 2018, Trump signed an Executive Order to set this plan in motion by pursuing every option available: challenge old court decisions; write regulations; and pass new laws.

This sent chills down my spine. We all know the history of the World War Two internment camps for Japanese-American families. Here was the President of the United States, surrounded by legislators and the press, proposing a similar strategy for refugee families.

We can get a good idea of what these internment camps for the long-term lockup of families would look like by examining the camps we already have. There are three of them: Dilley and Karnes in Texas and Berks in Pennsylvania. The difference is that these camps are restricted under current law, in most situations, from holding children for more than a few weeks.

It was time to hit the road to check them out. I was joined on this journey by Senators Mazie Hirono of Hawaii and Tina Smith of Minnesota, and Congresswoman Judy Chu from California.

It was a cold, dry, and windy day when we arrived at Dilley. Officially, this camp is called a "family residential center." Words can be used to soften or to sanitize an activity. The government uses the word "shelter" for prisons that lock up migrant children. And it uses the words "residential centers" for prisons for migrant families. I call them "internment camps," because they resemble the internment camps where we locked up Japanese-American families in World War Two. Senator Hirono was struck by that similarity. "It's terrible," she said. "This is what the internment camps looked like, if you look at the old internment camp grounds."

It is a sparse, sprawling facility that looks arid and uncomfortable. The family facilities are mobile trailer units. The sound of the wind beating against the walls of the trailers reinforced how desolate and unworldly this place is.

Most families at the camp were imprisoned there for less than three weeks under existing law, but some families were there much longer, caught in a complex web of immigration regulations. That was the case with Elena, who along with her daughter Carolina, had been locked up at Dilley for more than six months. (I have changed their names to protect them from an ongoing threat against their lives.) Elena had run a beauty shop back in Honduras and paid extortion to a local gang, as do virtually all businesses in the Northern Triangle. But the day came when she ran out of money and couldn't make the payment. The gang came to her house, held a gun to her head and another gun to her daughter's head. The gang then sexually assaulted Carolina as they forced Elena to watch. Elena and Carolina fled to the United States.

In the U.S., Elena tried to file for asylum. She couldn't find pro bono legal help, so she hired a lawyer. That lawyer took her money but paid little attention to the case. He filed an asylum petition for Elena but not for Carolina. And he didn't do the work necessary to properly prepare for the asylum hearing. Thus, he told her she would lose and withdrew her application for asylum. Without an asylum case pending, there was nothing to block ICE from moving forward with an order for deportation. ICE agents came to her house, arrested Elena and Carolina, and took them to Dilley to await the completion of transportation arrangements for a return to Honduras.

Elena's lawyer then said he would file a petition to reopen their asylum case, which would have stayed their deportation, but he failed to do it. Consequently, once the travel arrangements were in place, ICE woke them in the middle of the night, dragged them both from their room, and sent them to Houston for a flight out. Carolina, however, had a massive panic attack because of her profound fear of returning to Honduras where she was sure she would be raped or killed. They missed the flight, and the ICE agents took them back to

Dilley, where they were both placed in solitary confinement for a week as punishment.

At this point Elena and Carolina were trapped between a rock and a hard place. They didn't dare return to Honduras. And they couldn't bear to be locked up forever. A lawyer with the Dilley Pro Bono Project, Shay Fluharty, stepped in to assist them. Fluharty filed a Motion to Reopen each of their asylum claims. She won the motion for Carolina but not for Elena. In theory, Carolina could have been released from Dilley to stay with a sponsor for the continuation of her immigration proceedings, but her mother would have had to stay locked up. Carolina was concerned about being separated from her mother, whom she had never been apart from. In addition, she didn't have a suitable individual to serve as a sponsor. So they stayed at Dilley imprisoned together.

This was the situation when I met with Elena at Dilley. She cried through the entirety of our conversation. She told me that her daughter wasn't eating or sleeping right and had been suicidal. She was desperate. We were in Dilley on a Friday. I found out from Elena that her daughter's 15th birthday was the following Tuesday. A 15th birthday—the Quinceañera—is a big deal in Latin culture. I asked the prison administrator to host a Quinceañera party for Carolina. The answer was "no" because it was policy to not hold anything special for any one child. I then suggested that they hold a Quinceañera for each and every girl who turned 15 at Dilley. The answer was "no" because they said it wasn't acceptable to celebrate one culture over another. So I then suggested they hold a birthday party for every child of any age and any culture. The administrator said that was worth considering. The next week I got an email that said that they had considered the suggestion and were rejecting it. Too much work, apparently. Their decision shows how humanity dies at these prisons.

I decided if Dilley wouldn't celebrate her birthday, I would. My team made up a large card for Carolina—about a foot by two feet—that opened up with a sweet message wishing her a happy Quinceañera. I took it to the Tuesday lunch meeting of Democratic Senators and about 35 signed it. We then filmed a little video wishing her a happy birthday and emailed it to Fluharty, her lawyer. It took a few days before Fluharty could show her the video, but at least she knew that someone outside the prison was celebrating her.

Elena and Carolina are now out of prison, but not because they have won their asylum cases. Elena found Carolina trying to hang herself with a sheet in a bathroom at Dilley. Fluharty filed a complaint with the Office for Civil Rights and Civil Liberties at DHS explaining the circumstances and the risk to Carolina's life. ICE released them two days later, and they are working to establish an ordinary life in a city. Carolina is now in school, learning English, and playing soccer. In short, she is where a child should be: in a home and school rather than locked up in prison. Meanwhile, her and her mom's immigration cases continue; if they lose, they still face deportation.

73

I just pray and hope that Carolina can recover and thrive despite all the hardships she has gone through.

Elena and Carolina's story has elements that appear in the experiences of many refugees from Central America: fleeing violence; difficulty finding legal help to negotiate the American asylum process; and fly-by-night lawyers who make everything worse. And this: the stress and desperation that come from being locked up in a family prison. Meanwhile Dilley remains open, and the Trump administration is hard at work trying to create a massive system of family internment camps.

*   *   *

Once Judge Sabraw ordered an end to child separations, Trump and his team moved quickly to develop a plan to lock families up together. By watching Trump's press conference to announce his new plan, however, one might have thought Trump himself, rather than Judge Sabraw, had put an end to the child separations: "I didn't like the sight or the feeling of families being separated," Trump said. "I think the word 'compassion' comes into it." Trump recounted that Ivanka had shown him images of children in detention facilities and urged him to end child separation. "Ivanka feels very strongly, my wife feels very strongly, I feel very strongly," Trump said. "Anybody with a heart would feel strongly about it."[1]

While Trump was extolling compassion for migrant children at his press conference, the document he was announcing to the world—his new Executive Order (EO)—was anything but compassionate. The goal of the EO was to take children who were awaiting their asylum hearing in state-licensed facilities or sponsors' homes and throw them into prison along with their parents. The EO stated that it is "the policy of this administration to maintain family unity, including by detaining alien families together." Trump's EO then ordered the Secretary of Defense and the heads of all executive departments to make available any appropriate facilities "for the housing and care of alien families" and for the Department of Defense to "construct such facilities if necessary."[2]

Family internment camps. That was Trump's big idea. And it's a terrible idea. "This executive order effectively creates family prisons, which we already know are a threat to the well-being of children," observed Michelle Brané, Director of the Migrant Rights and Justice Program at the Women's Refugee Commission.[3] "The president doesn't get any brownie points for moving from a policy of locking up kids and families separately to a policy of locking them up together," said Karen Tumlin, Director of Legal Strategy at the National Immigration Law Center. "Let's be clear: Trump is making a crisis of his own creation worse."[4]

Trump was planning to lock up migrant families "throughout the pendency of criminal proceedings...or other immigration proceedings."[5] In other words, the families would be in family internment camps until the final resolution of their immigration cases, which could take years. Picture Elena and Carolina being sent back to Dilley.

But he faced a legal problem: the 1997 Flores Settlement Agreement (Flores).

Flores resolved a class-action lawsuit by setting standards for the detention and release of children in the custody of the former Immigration and Naturalization Service (INS), now DHS and HHS. The provisions included standards for the prison facilities such as safety, quality of drinking water and food, medical assistance, supervision, visitation, recreation, education, and counseling.[6]

It required the U.S. government "to treat all minors in its custody with dignity, respect, and special concern for their particular vulnerability as minors" and to detain each child "in the least restrictive setting appropriate to the minor's age and special needs."[7]

In keeping with the requirement for "the least restrictive setting," Flores required the swift transfer of children out of secure or unlicensed prisons to a sponsor or an unsecure state-licensed care facility. It set a maximum timeline for this transfer of three days for most CBP or ICE facilities and up to five days if the child was apprehended in a remote location.

In the case of an emergency or an "influx" of children to the United States, Flores provides some flexibility, requiring that children be transferred "as expeditiously as possible." When the court asked the Obama administration how long was reasonable in these situations, they suggested 20 days. That suggestion stuck. The maximum allowable period of imprisonment for a child under Flores is commonly specified as 20 days.

Flores creates a real obstacle for the Trump administration's plan to establish internment camps for the long-term imprisonment of migrant families. Flores requires that children be transferred to facilities within a 20-day period that are "non-secure" and "state-licensed," but a family internment camp cannot meet either of these conditions. States do not generally provide licenses for family detention. And since the administration wants to restrict the movement of the families, their internment camps would need to be secure.

The Trump administration was not following the Flores requirements rigorously, often holding children for more than 20 days. A nonprofit advocacy group, the Center for Human Rights and Constitutional Law, challenged this practice. The case went before U.S. District Judge Dolly Gee in the Central District Court of California. Her ruling was clear: Dilley, Karnes, and Berks were in violation of Flores.[8] The U.S. government could hold children at these secure, unlicensed facilities for up to 20 days "in the event of an emergency or influx of minors into the United States," but no longer.

This decision makes it clear that the U.S. cannot keep migrant families locked up. The Trump administration continues to try to find ways around Flores, however. In October 2018, the *Washington Post* reported that the White House was actively considering a plan "for the government to detain asylum-seeking families together for up to 20 days, then give parents a choice—stay in family detention with their child for months or years as their immigration case proceeds, or allow children to be taken to a government shelter so other relatives or guardians can seek custody."[9]

Under this "choose your trauma" approach, the U.S. government would make a mother or father decide between inflicting trauma on their child by choosing child separation, or by committing their child to indefinite imprisonment in a family internment camp. This idea is morally bankrupt, like asking a parent to choose between burning or beating their child. There is also a reasonable chance that the court would find that Flores blocks this option. It is not established that a parent can waive the requirement Flores imposes on the government to expeditiously transfer a child out of secure unlicensed prisons to a sponsor or state-licensed facility.

There is, therefore, only one way for the administration to establish a vast system of family internment camps. It must strike down Flores. That is exactly the goal of Trump's EO. It fires up three strategies for ending Flores: reverse Flores in court; replace Flores by publishing rules; or persuade Congress to pass a law to override Flores.

To challenge Flores in court, Trump ordered Jeff Sessions to file a petition with Judge Gee requesting that the court modify Flores to allow the long-term imprisonment of migrant families. The odds of Judge Gee modifying Flores in this fashion are low, for the same reason that Flores set standards in the first place: imprisonment is harmful to children and this harm makes it morally and legally unacceptable.

DHS and HHS put the second option in gear by publishing a proposed rule, utilizing a clause in Flores that states that the Flores Settlement Agreement will "terminate forty-five days after publication of final regulations implementing the agreement."[10]

But the problem for the administration is that its proposed rule doesn't "implement" Flores' requirements, it changes them. Most significantly, it replaces required state licensing and oversight with self-licensing and oversight. And because the proposed rule alters core principles of Flores, the replacement of Flores by this rule will almost certainly be challenged in court. In addition, Philip Wolgin, Managing Director on Immigration Policy at the Center for American Progress, argues that having ICE oversee its own facilities is a bad idea because the DHS Inspector General found that ICE has a poor track record on monitoring its facilities.[11]

Wolgin also observes that because the cost of the new regulation would be massive, at $2 billion to $12.9 billion over a ten-year period, it will trigger a Government Accountability Office (GAO) analysis under the "major rule" requirement of the Congressional Review Act. This creates a significant additional hurdle for this strategy.[12]

That leaves the third option: legislative action. This is the option Trump was really counting on. To emphasize the need for legislation, Trump titled his Executive Order "Affording Congress an Opportunity to Address Family Separation." At the press conference where he signed and publicized his plan surrounded by members of Congress, he said, "I'll be doing something that's somewhat preemptive and ultimately will be matched by legislation I'm sure."[13] To get the legislation done, Trump needed to move quickly. It seemed possible that Republicans could lose control of the House and possibly the Senate in the November election, and there was no way that a Congress controlled by Democrats was going to authorize a massive system of family internment camps.

Trump's team had already been working to lay the foundation for the legislation. A week earlier, Senator Chuck Grassley, then Chair of the Senate Judiciary Committee, tweeted, "I want 2 stop the separation of families at the border by repealing the Flores 1997 court decision requiring separation of families + give DOJ the tools it needs 2 quickly resolve cases."[14]

The House quickly took up the President's challenge. The day after Trump issued his EO, the House voted on the "Securing America's Future Act." This act was an extensive rewrite of immigration laws. It included the elimination of visas for family reunification; an indefinite extension of legal limbo for Dreamers—children who were brought to the U.S. and have grown up in America; and the elimination of protections for refugees seeking asylum. It would also have wiped out Flores, instructing DHS to "detain the alien with the alien's child."[15] The bill was voted down, with all Democrats and 41 Republicans voting against it.

Six days later, the House leadership tried again, putting the "Border Security and Immigration Reform Act" on the floor. This bill also had a broad set of modifications to immigration law that included reversing Flores, but it failed by an even larger margin: 112 Republicans joined all Democrats in defeating it.

The Senate was at work as well. Senator Ted Cruz of Texas was the first to act. On the day before Trump's press conference to announce his Executive Order to end Flores, Cruz introduced the "Protect Kids and Parents Act." His version of "protecting" children was to require the U.S. government to imprison migrant children and parents together. Senator Thom Tillis of North Carolina followed the next day with the "Keep Families Together and Enforce the Law Act." This bill would have legalized imprisonment of migrant families for the duration of their legal proceedings and authorized 1,000 additional prison beds for families. In addition to Tillis, the bill had 39 co-sponsors. This floored me. Forty members of the U.S. Senate had backed the creation of family internment camps for the long-term imprisonment of migrant children.

I went to the floor of the Senate to deliver an extensive speech reviewing our country's shameful history of internment camps for Japanese-Americans in World War Two and to declare that if either of the bills for expanding internment camps proceeded, I would organize an all-out campaign of opposition. I wanted to make it clear that this would be a massive fight. At least one Senator heard me that mattered: Tillis of North Carolina. By coincidence he was presiding over the Senate debate as I spoke. We never talked about it later, so I don't know if that coincidence changed his thinking on the issue. What I do know is that all momentum for these bills evaporated. Despite President Trump pressing hard for legislation, Senate Majority Leader McConnell did not move forward in trying to put either the Cruz or the Tillis bill on the floor.

The legislative battle then turned to the spending bills that are prepared by the Appropriations Committees of the House and Senate. Passage of these bills is required to keep the government open, so a provision inserted into one of them has a better chance to make it into law than a freestanding policy bill. In the House, Congressman Tom Cole worked successfully to insert an amendment to nullify Flores into the Labor, Health, and Human Services spending bill. The Cole Amendment succeeded by a 31-21 vote in committee.

I serve on the corresponding spending committee in the Senate and went to work to both block child separations and protect Flores. The result was extensive language in the Senate Committee Report expressing concern about child separation, supporting family reunification, and emphasizing the quick release of children from DHS facilities. The language restates the Flores requirement "that all UACs should be transferred from DHS to HHS within 72 hours and promptly placed in the least restrictive setting that is in the best interest of the child" and then "directs HHS to notify the Committee immediately should children remain in DHS custody longer than 72 hours before being transferred to HHS." When the House and the Senate spending bills were merged, the Cole Amendment was stripped out.[16]

*   *   *

It is reasonable to ask: If child separation and family imprisonment are both unacceptable, what is the best way to treat
migrant families seeking asylum? The answer is the Family
Case Management Program (FCMP).

When a family has a case manager who keeps the family
fully informed on how the asylum system works and why
and where they must show up, they do show up. This is the
best way to treat a migrant family with respect and dignity.
The family stays together. Children are able to be in homes,
schools, and playgrounds, which is where they should be.
And the families do show up for their immigration check-ins
and asylum hearings.

The pilot program assisted 800 families in five metro-
politan areas—New York / Newark, Washington, D.C. /
Baltimore, Los Angeles, Miami, and Chicago. ICE's own
report evaluating the program found an average 99.4 percent attendance for check-ins and a 99.3 percent attendance
at court hearings.[17] This is a very different picture from the
President's description of "catch and release," in which families rarely show up for check-ins and hearings.

In addition to excellent attendance results, FCMP costs
far less per family than prisons. FCMP costs approximately
$38 each day per family unit.[18] By contrast, holding a fam-
ily in Dilley or Karnes costs nearly $320 per person each
day.[19] If an average family has two to three members, the

apples-to-apples comparison would be $38 for FCMP, and $640–960 for a family internment camp. To put it another way, family management is 17 to 25 times cheaper than family imprisonment.

The Trump administration canceled this program in June 2017. Given its effectiveness and low cost, why would they do that? I think that the Trump team did not want the evidence that there was an excellent alternative to either child separation or family imprisonment. So they killed the program.

A similar approach to FCMP can work for individuals. One such program—Intensive Supervision Appearance—used either technology like ankle bracelets or full-service case managers, depending on the situation. The U.S. Government Accountability Office reports that migrants in the full-service program had a 99 percent appearance rate at their court hearings, and the program cost an average of just $10.55 a day per person.[20]

Bottom line: Immigrants show up when they have a case manager helping them through a complicated and confusing system that might just help them out of the chaos of their lives.

SIX

AMERICAN GULAG

FEW PLACES REFLECT THE DYSFUNCTION AND HORROR OF THE American child immigration system like Tornillo. The Trump administration established Tornillo in mid-June 2018, as a temporary influx facility for migrant youth 13 to 17 years old. By December it had become the largest facility detaining children in U.S. history—a symbol of America's mass incarceration of refugee children. I headed there with the same congressional team that had visited the internment camps—Senators Mazie Hirono and Tina Smith, along with Congresswoman Judy Chu. Congressman Beto O'Rourke of Texas joined us when we arrived. It was December 15, ten days before Christmas 2018.

Tornillo was built like a refugee camp, with smaller tents housing boys staked out in rows, interspersed with larger tents housing the girls and providing common facilities like the dining room. Children clothed in government-issued pants and shirts were marched from place to place in single-file lines with staff in front and staff behind. The beds were made in immaculate military style. In the girls' dormitory tent, every bed had a teddy bear placed in exactly the same place. The children were not allowed to touch each other: no hand holding, no hugging, no contact. The camp felt sterile and almost soulless.

Tornillo was a secure facility, with fences and barbwire preventing children from leaving. It didn't have a state license to operate as a child care facility, and therefore wasn't subject to state requirements for caring for children or to state inspections. It was up to ORR to provide guidelines for how they wanted the camp operated. There was no state requirement, for example, for providing an education to the children.

Our delegation to the camp was met by Kevin Dinnin, CEO of the nonprofit BCFS Health and Human Services, which was under contract to establish and operate the camp. During our tour, we had many opportunities to ask him questions. And I greatly appreciate that he was the one person in the immigration system who really worked at giving honest answers and assessments.

One issue I was concerned about was how long children were being held at the camp. Since Tornillo was established as an influx facility to accommodate a temporary surge in migrants, it seemed like children would be kept a short time before being moved to state-licensed facilities or sponsors' homes. Moreover, since Tornillo was a secure, unlicensed facility, it would seem that Flores would require that children not be held there for more than 20 days. Despite that, I had heard that Flores was not being rigorously followed, and that some children had been there for longer periods of time. So I asked Dinnin: "I've heard that there are a few kids here over the 20-day limit, is that true? Are there a few dozen children in that situation?"

"Oh my," he replied, "the number is far more than that. Over half the children have been here over 20 days."

We were shocked. Then I asked how long the child held longest had been there. His reply: "About five months, almost from when we opened." A child had been held locked up behind barbwire at Tornillo for roughly 150 days. So much for the Flores limit of 20 days.

Why was this the case? ORR told Dinnin that Flores had special allowances as an influx shelter and did not provide any guidelines to BCFS limiting how long children could be kept there. They just kept sending him more children with requests for expanding the size of the camp. We heard from some that Tornillo was exempted from Flores because it was a temporary facility. And that it maintained its temporary status by not hooking up to the electric grid or the municipal water system. Electricity was provided by diesel generators and water was brought in by potable water trucks from a nearby fire hydrant. This was partly true.

BCFS did use generators and truck in water, but did so because the local utilities were inadequate, not because it would exempt Tornillo from Flores.

Based on conversations with immigration lawyers and

advocates, we learned that the real reason Tornillo didn't abide by the Flores 20-day limit is it wasn't asked to do so. An issue related to the enforcement of the 20-day limit has to be put before Judge Gee, who oversees the implementation of Flores. The Center for Human Rights and Constitutional Law, the lead counsel for Flores, has asked the court to address the 20-day limit in the context of the family internment camps like Dilley and Karnes, but it has not put the same issue before the court in the context of migrant child influx prisons like Tornillo. I asked Peter Schey, the Executive Director of the center about how this works. He indicated that they did plan to take this issue to Judge Gee in the future, but hadn't had the time or resources to do so yet. As long as ORR has not been explicitly instructed by the court to adhere to the 20-day limit, ORR is happy to ignore it.

Tornillo was established at the same time the administration was starting its child separation policy. The message from ORR was that if there wasn't an influx facility for these children, the children would be stuck under terrible conditions at CBP *hieleras* or holding cages for longer periods of time. But the number of children locked up in the system of migrant child prisons started to grow way faster than explained by the child separations. Why? It wasn't the number of children coming into the system. Ten thousand more children were referred to ORR in 2016 than in 2018. The answer is in how many children were moved out of the system and placed with sponsors. In 2018, ORR placed only

35,000 children with sponsors as compared to the 49,100 children they took in, causing number of children in the ORR gulag to surge.[1]

What was going on? Why did ORR release so few children to sponsors? In a word, fingerprints.

The administration started requiring that every person in a potential sponsor's household be fingerprinted while at the same time they were sharing the information from sponsors' applications with ICE. There was no surer way to discourage a family from serving as a sponsor than to threaten them with special attention from ICE, which might lead to the arrest and deportation of family members. With fewer sponsors, children moved out of the migrant child gulag more slowly, so the total number of children locked up grew quickly.

This was not the only choke point in the system. The FBI needed more resources to examine and clear the fingerprints. The child prisons needed more caseworkers to contact and arrange sponsors. And ORR needed more federal fieldworkers to sign off on the sponsor placements, as well as more staff at General Dynamics Information Technology (GDIT), a third-party contractor that also has to sign off on sponsor placements.

And then, even when the sponsors' applications were complete, the administration was sitting on some of the applications rather than releasing the children to the sponsors. It is hard to explain exactly why this was happening, but Dinnin put it to us bluntly:

"I could get 1,300 of these children into sponsors' homes in short order if the administration would release the children who already have sponsors with completed applications."

Tornillo had been opened with a vision of housing between 400 and 500 children. But by the time we arrived, the count was up to about 2,800 children and the average stay had climbed to more than 50 days. Many children there had been held at other facilities before arriving at Tornillo.

One Guatemalan girl, age 16, told NBC News that she had been at Tornillo for a month after spending two and a half months at another facility in Miami. She hoped to be reunited with her brother in Texas. It makes no sense that she couldn't have been placed with a sponsor in a three-and-a-half-month period. And it makes no sense that she couldn't have had an asylum conference with an asylum officer in such a long period to even see if she would qualify for asylum.[2] To get that story, the NBC correspondent had to sneak in a side conversation with the teenager while the reporter was on a tour of the facility, because the press was banned from having direct conversations with the children. Such conversations were banned during our visit as well. Our ability to converse was limited to saying "hello" or asking "Where are you from?" as children passed by in a line. How can members of Congress exercise oversight if they aren't able to talk to children about what they are experiencing?

A 17-year-old boy from Honduras, who had recently been released from Tornillo, spoke to an Associated Press reporter about how indefinite incarceration preys on the children's spirits: "The few times they let me call my mom I would tell her that one day I would be free, but really I felt like I would be there for the rest of my life. I feel so bad for the kids who are still there. What if they have to spend Christmas there? They need a hug, and nobody is allowed to hug there."[3]

Operating Tornillo was expensive. BCFS estimates that it cost $750 a day to house a child. That meant it was burning taxpayer funds at a rate of more than $2 million per day when we visited. Dinnin observes that soft-side facilities are much more expensive than brick and mortar sites because of the huge expense of renting all the tents and the equipment that goes into them. Public advocates pointed out several concerns about the operation of Tornillo. Perhaps the most significant concern was that the Director of ORR had waived background checks for child abuse and neglect for the more than 2,000 staff members hired since Tornillo opened. BCFS ran its own background checks through a private contractor, but these are a poor substitute for the more powerful searches possible through the FBI system or the Texas state system.

BCFS wanted to have access to the FBI system for background checks, but they were turned down. Apparently a private company cannot under current law use the FBI vendors to run names through the National Crime Information Center (NCIC) database, even when the company is under contract to the U.S. government. At one point, HHS arranged for CBP to set up a team on-site to provide this function for BCFS, but CBP canceled the plan at the last moment citing legal concerns. Finally, by November, five months after Tornillo opened, ORR was able to work out an arrangement with the Texas Department of Public Safety to run the background checks. This is obviously a problem that needs to be fixed going forward.

Another concern was a reported shortage of mental health professionals. The federal standard for facilities that care for migrant children is one mental health clinician for every 12 kids, but ORR set a much lower standard for Tornillo of one for every 67 children.[4]

ORR argued that the lower standard was acceptable because the children sent to Tornillo had undergone a mental health screening at other facilities and that only children without special needs were being sent to Tornillo. Dinnin noted that BCFS strived to do better than the minimum standard set by ORR even as Tornillo expanded rapidly, reaching an average ratio of one mental health clinician to 39 children. This remains an area of concern, however, because there has been little transparency or oversight of ORR's procedures and judgment. And mental health clinicians note that mental health challenges might be hard to spot in a screening and that incarceration itself introduces additional stresses that can create or amplify mental health issues.

As we left Tornillo we met with the press outside the gates. With more than a dozen cameras rolling, we called for two things: First, for President Trump to release all the children who already had sponsors lined up. And second, for ORR to shut down Tornillo and the other influx camp at Homestead Air Base in Florida. Back at Congress, Representative Chu and I introduced the "Shut Down Child Prison Camps Act," with the goal of shuttering both Tornillo and Homestead.

Miraculously, the Trump administration did act. Right before Christmas, they announced they were releasing 4,000 children to their sponsors. That's a lot of children celebrating the holidays in homes and schools and playgrounds rather than at a prison or detention facility. And ORR also announced that it was considering shutting down Tornillo, and it did so in January.

It appears that the shutdown resulted from pressure both within and outside the system. From the outside, intense public scrutiny and criticism were creating extensive pressure to close the camp. From inside, Kevin Dinnin, the CEO of BCFS, was deeply disturbed at the situation. "The children were coming in but never leaving," he said. "We as an organization finally drew the line. You can't keep taking children in and not releasing them."[5] BCFS declined the opportunity to extend the contract and no other contractors stepped in to take it over. Tornillo is closed. And that's a good thing.

Even as HHS announced in December that they were considering closing Tornillo, they were preparing to double the capacity of Homestead from 1,350 to 2,350. Four months later, DHS announced another expansion, to 3,200 beds. HHS attributed the expansion to a dramatic spike in unaccompanied children arriving at the border.

This time, there was a spike in migrants arriving on the border; a spike generated directly by President Trump. When Trump announced in October 2018 that he was considering using a national emergency to marshal more resources to block migrants from coming to the United States, he created a powerful incentive for individuals and families suffering violence or oppression to travel north while it was possible. That incentive was amplified by his actual declaration of an emergency on February 15, 2019. According to some reports, coyotes—the smugglers who escort migrants—used his announcements to advertise for customers, further increasing the response. As a result, the number of refugees coming to the border, as measured by CBP's apprehensions, climbed quickly. In September 2018: 50,568. In February 2019: 76,535. And in March 2019: 103,492.

I visited Homestead as it was growing in early 2019 to see for myself how they were managing so many children in prison.

Homestead is located at the Homestead Air Reserve Base. Like Tornillo, it doesn't have a state license. As a brick-and-mortar facility it looks very different from Tornillo, but its internal functioning is much the same. One big operational difference, however, is that it is operated by a for-profit company: Comprehensive Health Services (CHS).

One of the mysteries is how Homestead keeps order with so many stressed children.

"How do you enforce discipline?" I asked Leslie Wood, Program Director of Homestead. "You have all these kids from a variety of traumatic backgrounds. They are probably pretty stressed about their status, and have a fair amount of anxiety about what lies ahead. It seems like there would be a fair amount of disciplinary challenges in that."

I knew from earlier reports that there were concerns about Homestead using solitary confinement to discipline children. Not least because children used to walk around the prison wearing name tags that said "soli" on them. Those name tags disappeared when people started to ask questions.

Wood insisted that they never used solitary confinement except if there was a health issue like a child with a fever.

"In order to keep them in line, do you ever tell them they won't be able to leave the facility or get a placement with a sponsor if they misbehave?" I asked.

"Never," she said. "I would fire anybody who told that to a child."

Later on our tour of the prison, we were permitted to talk to three teenage boys who are part of the student government. I asked them if anybody ever said that if they misbehaved, it could affect their ability to leave here and be placed with a sponsor family.

All three of them immediately said, "Si, si, si."

I turned to the director. "You said you didn't do it, but all the boys just said absolutely yes. So how do you reconcile what you told me and what the boys told me?"

"Well it's true," she admitted. "If somebody misbehaves

in a significant and serious way, it could affect their ability to be placed with a family. That is just the reality. If they have anger management problems or start a fight, it could affect their ability to be placed. We're just telling them the honest truth." The conversation reinforced how hard it is to get a straight answer from many officials in the immigration system.

I asked how long the children are held at Homestead, wondering if Homestead came closer than Tornillo to respecting the Flores 20-day standard. The answer is no. At the time we visited, the average stay for a child was about two months. That is the average; many children have been locked up there for much longer.

There is another concern about Homestead. It sits at a site in Florida vulnerable to hurricanes. A Category Two storm could generate a six-foot wave hitting Homestead. Does Homestead have a complete evacuation plan ready? How will they get enough buses or planes to evacuate more than 3,000 children? Where will the children go? Wood tells me that a full plan is ready. Advocates believe that there is not a complete and adequate plan in place and that ORR is scrambling to figure out where and how to evacuate the children, even as another hurricane season is upon us. I hope the advocates are wrong.

Another concern is the for-profit status of the operator, CHS, a subsidiary of Caliburn International. CHS presents a fundamental conflict of interest. It makes money by keeping children locked up at its facility, even as it has the responsibility of expediting the transfer of children to state-licensed care facilities and sponsors. Thus, if it hires more caseworkers to get children placed more quickly with sponsors, which is what it should be doing, it loses money.

I'm deeply disturbed that in April 2019, former DHS Secretary John Kelly took a paid position on Caliburn's board. Before he was DHS Secretary, John Kelly sat on the board of a private equity firm, DC Capital Partners. In March 2017, just as Kelly as Secretary of DHS was cranking up the child separation strategy that would drive more children into CHS facilities, Kelly's former firm bought CHS. In August 2018, Kelly's former firm formed a new company, Caliburn, by combining CHS and three other companies.[6] Now that Kelly is out of office, he is rewarded with a paid position on the Caliburn board, having supported and implemented policies in office that made DC Capital Partners and Caliburn a lot of money from the business of imprisoning children for profit. It is hard to imagine that CHS, under Caliburn's direction, will expedite the transfer of children to sponsors or state-licensed facilities, even though that is their responsibility. It is way past time for the oversight of Flores to be applied aggressively to Homestead.

* * *

The large majority of the migrant children locked up by the U.S. government are held in state-licensed detention centers. The numbers have gone up and down. The combined total for the influx prisons and the detention centers hit a peak of nearly 15,000 in December 2018, and then dropped to 11,000 when ORR released 4,000 children right before Christmas. As of May 2019, the number was back near record highs, with over 13,000 children locked up.[7]

The largest facility is Casa Padre, where I tried unsuccessfully to get in on June 3, 2018. That visit created an uproar, and the press were given a tour ten days later. I then returned on Father's Day, June 17, with a congressional delegation including Senator Chris Van Hollen and Representatives Filemon Vela, Vicente Gonzalez, and Sheila Jackson-Lee of Texas, Peter Welch of Vermont, Mark Pocan of Wisconsin, and David Cicilline of Rhode Island. The doors were wide open this time, and the CEO of Southwest Key, Juan Sanchez, was there to show us around.

When I first went to Southwest Key, immigrant advocates told me that hundreds of boys were locked up there, maybe as many as a thousand. I mentioned this on Facebook Live, and then regretted saying it, because I was sure that it couldn't be true that 1,000 boys had been stuffed into a single former Walmart store. The immigrant advocates were wrong. There weren't 1,000 boys in there; there were almost 1,500! It sounded like something out of a Charles Dickens novel—it couldn't be possible. But it was.

Southwest Key started to get a lot of public criticism for having boys locked up at Casa Padre after my first visit. I received several calls from leaders in the Hispanic community who told me that Sanchez was an upstanding member of the community and was doing great work providing excellent care for the migrant children as they awaited placements with sponsors. They told me that Juan Sanchez and Southwest Key were heroes, not villains. And they were concerned that stories about the children imprisoned at Casa Padre might lead to staff or the children getting hurt by angry protestors.

In response to these calls, I did try to focus public attention on the immoral Trump child separation policy, rather than specifically on Casa Padre. And I organized a call to talk with Sanchez and some of the other board members.

On that call, as I listened to Sanchez tell me how much he and Southwest Key did to watch out for the children's welfare, there was one thing that bothered me. No one from Southwest Key had expressed concern about Trump's child separation policy. As experts working with children, surely they were aware of the trauma that policy was causing. Surely, as child advocates, they would speak up about it.

"Look, you say you are a champion for children," I said. "So why don't you publicly protest this child separation policy? You see the impact firsthand. You can be an effective voice pushing the government."

"If we do that, we might lose our contracts," Sanchez replied.

"So why don't you call up the heads of the other nonprofits providing services to migrant children and write a letter of protest together with them? The government can't target all of you; they need your resources and expertise."

He said he would look into that. When I visited Casa Padre a few days later, I asked if he had followed up. He hadn't.

Casa Padre had expanded explosively. Southwest Key had

built 300 bedrooms inside the former Walmart. Sanchez told me that in February they had 300 boys, in March 500 boys, and now almost 1,500. The bedrooms went from one boy each to five boys each. The boys are between 10 and 17 in age. Younger boys are sent to different facilities.

Because Casa Padre was licensed by the state of Texas, Southwest Key had to get plans for this expansion approved. I wonder how thorough the review process was.

I asked Sanchez about the consequences of the rapid expansion. "What were the logistical challenges? What do you most need that you don't have?"

I was expecting him to talk about hiring cooks or ordering groceries, but his reply took me aback. He said the biggest challenge was mental health counselors.

"Well how many are you short?" I asked.

"About ninety," he said.

"That's a ton. How are you going about hiring them?"

"We're really working hard to hire them," Sanchez said. "We went to Puerto Rico because we need Spanish-language counselors, and quite frankly it's quite hard to persuade counselors to transfer here. They're happily employed where they are."

His response made me once again conclude that the Trump administration's planning for the launch of their Zero Tolerance policy was woefully inadequate. They knew that the Zero Tolerance plan would cause a massive surge in the number of boys held in a place like this. They knew that these were children who were fleeing persecution and that the journey north often included more suffering. And they knew that their child separation strategy would inflict more trauma. Surely counselors were one of the things that they would plan for. But they didn't.

The counselor shortage symbolized for me the Trump administration's lack of concern for the welfare of these children. The administration has been driven by a political objective—deterring immigration—while ignoring the impact of their tactics: trauma to children. So they stuffed the boys into some building somewhere. It was still astonishing to me that there were 1,500 boys imprisoned in that former Walmart.

The hallways of Casa Padre featured murals of presidents and inspirational quotes, and the first mural features President Trump against the backdrop of an American flag. Beside his black-and-white image is a quote from his book, *The Art of the Deal*: "Sometimes by losing a battle you find a new way to win the war." The quote next to the image of Barack Obama was a stark contrast. It was taken from a 2014 speech announcing protections for undocumented immigrants: "My fellow Americans, we are and always will be a nation of immigrants. We were strangers once, too."

In what was previously a McDonald's within the Walmart, the prison workers served meals of chicken and vegetables.[8] Children watched movies in what used to be loading docks. A handful of them played basketball in a former garage. According to the staff, new boys arrived from the border each day in vans. They spent their first few days getting checked out for medical problems and vaccinated.

There were so many boys here that Southwest Key needs to have two shifts for school: one in the morning and one in the afternoon. The boys were allowed outside two hours each day, and could make two phone calls a week. It could take days, or even weeks, for the children to talk to their parents.[9]

Sanchez showed us around their outdoor activity area, their game room, and a video room. I couldn't stop wondering how long it would take 1,500 boys to share a soccer field. If 20 boys played at once for a one-hour game, they would need to be on the field for three days and nights solid before they all got to play. Inside the game room there was a broken foosball table. Even if it were fixed, how long would it take for 1,500 boys to cycle through one foosball table?

As we walked through the former Walmart store, Sanchez told us they were the good guys in all this. They were in the business of doing good by the children. These children needed to be cared for. They were doing the right thing by giving them the best care they could, he explained.

Sanchez also objected to me calling the place a child prison or detention center.

"No, no," he said, "we are a shelter."

"Well, a shelter is some place you go because you want to go there," I explained. "It's not some place you're forced to go to. It's a place where you can leave if you want."

"The kids could leave," he replied. "We don't have barbwire around the fence."

That's not how the children viewed it. They had no choice: They had to be there. Many were hoping for the news that they would be released to a sponsor, in most cases a relative. They certainly did not believe that they were allowed to walk out the front door, because they weren't.

Sanchez grew up in Brownsville, in a poor family, but worked his way to having three degrees, including one from Harvard. He set up his own nonprofit, now headquartered in Austin. According to Sanchez and his supporters, he is an advocate for social justice. His organization was also detaining more migrant children than anyone in the nation, with 5,000 children in 24 detention facilities. His nonprofit earns hundreds of millions of dollars in federal contracts.

After our visit, reporters began to look into the operation of Southwest Key. What they found wasn't pretty. The *New York Times* reported that in 2018 "Southwest Key paid eight people more than the federal salary cap of $187,000." Sanchez earned $1.5 million as CEO and his wife, Jennifer Sanchez, brought home $500,000 as a vice president. In addition, he had arranged insider deals with for-profit companies he has a stake in, squeezing even more personal profit out of the facilities.[10] This type of conflict is corrupt, pure and simple. If a company or a nonprofit is making millions off of housing migrant children, couldn't they do better than cramming 1,500 boys into a single former Walmart with inadequate play fields and a broken foosball table?

Nine months later, in March 2019, Sanchez stepped down as CEO, as the Department of Justice investigated the possible misuse of federal money. "Recent events have convinced me that Southwest Key would benefit from a fresh perspective and new leadership," he said in a statement. "Widespread misunderstanding of our business and unfair criticism of our people has become a distraction our employees do not deserve. It's time for new beginnings."[11]

* * *

In February 2019, Congressman Ted Deutch released documents from HHS detailing the extent of sexual assault cases on unaccompanied minors and separated children in ORR custody. According to the documents, more than one thousand allegations of sexual abuse on minors were reported to ORR each of the last two fiscal years. Of those, only forty-nine were reported to DOJ each year. "These HHS documents detail a staggering number of sexual assaults on unaccompanied children in their custody," Congressman Deutch said. "Together, these documents detail an unsafe environment of sexual assaults by staff on unaccompanied minors. With the number of allegations each year roughly breaking down to one sexual assault per week for the last three years, clearly this administration is not equipped to keep these children safe inside their facilities. Congress and the public demand answers and a clearer understanding of how these allegations are being investigated and what is being done to protect these vulnerable children."[12]

The following month, Senators Chuck Grassley and Dianne Feinstein requested the HHS Inspector General investigate "the alleged widespread and long-term pattern of sexual abuse against unaccompanied children" in the ORR-funded facilities. "Recent public reports allege that many cases of sexual assault in child care centers are not fully investigated by HHS," wrote Grassley and Feinstein. "We find it intolerable and inexcusable that child care operators are not immediately investigating reports, contacting and fully assisting law enforcement, preserving evidence, and demanding justice for these children."[13]

The Senators wanted to know, and all of us should want to know, if HHS and its contractors are following the best practices for handling sexual abuse allegations, and what can be done to stop the assaults and bring the perpetrators to justice. In one case in Arizona involving a Southwest Key facility in Youngtown, the County Sheriff deputies failed to interview either the facility's employees or the minors. This case and others prompted the Arizona Senate to approve legislation in March 2019 to improve the regulation of migrant youth facilities.[14] Those improvements included required reporting of child abuse allegations to a state registry and authority for state health regulators to inspect federal facilities that provide behavioral health services. The bill also requires background checks on staff, addressing a scandal in which it was discovered that Southwest Key failed to perform appropriate background checks on employees at facilities it operates in Arizona.

The HHS Inspector General spokeswoman has confirmed that the agency has a review of the ORR facilities underway, including how they identify and respond to sexual assault allegations.

It turns out that when thousands of traumatized children are imprisoned for political purposes, without regard for their welfare and without adequate planning, a lot of bad things happen. We shouldn't be surprised, but we should be outraged.

SEVEN

ARC OF MY JOURNEY

MY EYES WERE FIRST OPENED TO THE BROADER WORLD WHEN an exchange student walked into my sixth-grade classroom. She was from our local high school, but had spent her summer in Japan. She told stories that seemed to me, a blue-collar kid whose universe was our neighborhood and the wilds of Oregon, extraordinarily exotic. Different food, different customs, different language, different everything.

Each year our high school sent one student abroad through the AFS (American Field Service) student exchange program. Only one student was selected to go. And to get a shot at going, you needed to study a language for two years, not because AFS would send you to the country whose language you studied, but because it was a commitment to understanding other cultures. I knew at that moment, sitting in my sixth-grade classroom, that I would take those two years of language and apply. To be able to travel somewhere around the world ... Wow!

Five years later I was sitting in front of a woman who was interviewing me as a potential AFS student. She asked me where, if selected, would I like to go. I was confounded by the question, and responded that I had understood that you had no influence on where you were sent. You were signing up to go wherever AFS chose to send you.

"Yes that's true," the interviewer told me. "But I think it's always very interesting to hear what the applicants have to say."

"I'd like to go someplace that I'd never otherwise be able to go," I replied. "I don't want to go someplace like Europe because my impression is that it is much like America. I'd like to go somewhere entirely different, someplace I'd never otherwise be able to experience, somewhere like Africa."

The utterance of that word, "Africa," was to have a profound influence on my life.

Foreign travel was not a part of my world before I heard about AFS. I come from the small timber town of Myrtle Creek, Oregon. My father worked as a millwright—the mechanic who keeps the machines at the mill humming—at another mill down the road in Riddle. Those timber mills dotted the landscape in the first half of the 1900s, but in the 1950s they started to disappear. In some cases they ran out of timber. In many others, an investor or a larger company bought them out. And so it was that the mill shut down in Riddle and we moved to Roseburg, where my dad tried his hand at many different jobs from designing and building a rock crusher, to repairing logging machinery in the woods, to building houses.

With the economy hurting in Roseburg and my dad wanting to spend more time with his children, we moved again, this time to the much larger city of Portland where he located a machinist's position with regular hours.

In my office is a photo of my dad, standing like a daredevil on the seat of a motorbike as he rides down the street. The picture is all the more remarkable when you know that as a child he twice lost the use of his legs. Dad contracted tuberculosis from drinking unpasteurized milk on the farm. That type of tuberculosis attacks the bones; and in his case, attacked his spine. He lost the ability to walk as a toddler, recovered, and again lost the use of his legs when he was 14. His family sent him to a children's hospital run by the Mormon Church in Salt Lake City for "crippled children," as they called them at that time.

His stay at the hospital proved to be a blessing. The doctors tried an experimental surgery to repair his spine and it worked. And during the many months he spent recovering in bed in a turtle shell cast, he listened to world news on the radio and devoured books—as many as two a day—enabling him to learn much more about the world than he would have otherwise.

At the hospital he became well aware of the prejudices regarding "crippled" children, who were often treated in that day and age as third-class citizens. He believed in a God that loved all of creation equally, and he despised discrimination and bigotry wherever he found it. He would tell me how disgusted he was when he was aboard a bus that crossed from Arizona into Texas, and the driver stood up and announced that under Texas law, every Hispanic and African-American had to go to the back of the bus.

He was disturbed when he worked building a highway in Costa Rica during World War Two and discovered that the Hispanic Costa Ricans were paid one-tenth the wage of the white Americans. And he left the Mormon Church because at that time the church discriminated against dark-skinned individuals because they believed that dark skin was the mark of Cain—the biblical son of Adam and Eve who murdered his brother Abel—a source of impurity. From my father I took a fierce belief in the equality of all individuals and a determination that America should be a leader in the world in fighting discrimination and bigotry.

My mother's journey was no easier than dad's. Her mother had had a previous family of three. After her first husband abandoned the family, she hand-washed other families' clothes to get by. But things got so rough that, according to family lore, she spent time living in a boxcar. The county took her three children away, sending the two girls to an orphanage and the son to work on a farm, where he died from carbon monoxide poisoning from a kerosene heater.

My mother's father, Grandpa Collins, never had a real job. He kept the family afloat playing poker and making homebrew. He and Grandma Collins had four children together, with my mother being the oldest. Grandma Collins died when my mother was seven from an allergic response to anesthesia during a surgery. After she died the family piled into an open-top carriage car and headed for Arizona. Mom remembers a woman at a roadside motel finding some clothes to warm up the poor waifs in the car. When I read *The Grapes of Wrath*, I felt I was reading about my mother's family.

My mother had simple instructions for life: Do what's right. Do your best. And never ever step on anyone else to get ahead. She is meticulously honest. I recall her counting the change at the store and always handing back any extra a clerk had given her by mistake.

From my mother I learned the importance of treating everyone fairly and squarely. If my mother had ten minutes alone with Donald Trump, he might be a different man.

* * *

It was happening. I was 16, seated with five other American high school students sharing a Crossroads Africa charter plane filled with college students en route to Ghana. It was the only program AFS had in Africa outside of apartheid-era South Africa. My fellow AFS companions went to live with affluent Ghanaian host families in cities. My assignment was different.

My host family was in Tafo-Akim, a small town of a few thousand people. The town's defining feature was that it hosted the Cocoa Research Institute of Ghana, which was dedicated to studying and finding cures to diseases affecting

Ghana's cocoa industry. My host father was a public school-teacher with just a high school education himself. The mother taught at a Catholic school.

The government had built a neighborhood of concrete houses in support of the research institute, and my family benefited from one of them. It had three rooms: A sitting room in the middle with a bedroom on either side. A court-yard with a water pump that served as a kitchen. No bath-room, just an outhouse with a bucket under the seat. In the middle of the night, you could hear the dogs barking as a man swapped out buckets to take care of the "night soil."

The big feature of the house was electricity. The family had a lightbulb in the middle of each room and a single electric appliance: an iron. Each night my host father ironed every piece of clothing that his niece had washed that day. The other big luxury was a bicycle. No one got to ride that bicycle except the father.

At my first meal with the family, there was a strange-looking item sitting in the middle of a large bowl of ground-nut stew at the center of the table. It looked like a giant slug.

"What is that?" I asked.

"That's a delicacy and you must have it," the mother said as she flopped it into my bowl of starchy fufu. It wasn't a slug. It was a large tree snail, cooked without its shell. The Giant Ghana Snail is the largest land snail in the world, growing up to 12 inches long. My brain said "snail," but my mind saw slug. I couldn't eat it. I just couldn't rise to meet the challenge.

I was determined to right this wrong before I left Ghana: to eat one of those tree snails. But my host mother was not impressed. She said they were out of season, and that she would cook one only if I could find one, and she was pretty sure I couldn't.

But I had an idea how to do that. The father and I had visited a small village of about eight mud huts and thatched roofs where we had arranged for a man to weave some kente cloth, the beautiful strips of fabric that you sometimes see displayed like a scarf around the necks of African-American leaders. While we were there, I had noticed that one woman kept tree snails in a barrel. Maybe she still had one. After much cajoling, my host father let me borrow his bike to ride out to this village.

You can imagine how strange it was for folks in that small group of thatched homes to see this tall white guy ride up on a bicycle and start negotiating in Twi for a snail. She had one left, and I got it. I have a picture in which I am holding that cooked snail above my mouth right before I ate it, stuffing the whole thing in at once. Great preparation for *Fear Factor* or *Survivor*. It tasted like a clam: not bad. Mission accomplished.

My summer in Ghana had a profound impact on me. I was surrounded by folks who earned a few dollars a day. I talked with a father about the challenge of feeding his seven children. With a dollar a day he could buy one plantain for each child, and that was it. So his children, like the children in so many families, had to work rather than go to school. In the middle of town, children would swarm the buses to sell sweets or trinkets through the windows. Other children helped staff stalls in the marketplace or sold bread door-to-door. Life was hard. The children's opportunities were limited.

When I came back to Oregon I saw my home and family differently. When I left Oregon, my family had a simple home in a working neighborhood, definitely not on the affluent side of the railroad tracks. Upon return, I marveled at the wealth of my family. We had a house with a bedroom for each child, a basement, a television, multiple bicycles, a car, and a garage to keep it in. We were spectacularly well off!

* * *

From that summer came a powerful interest in the world, but I had no idea how that would fit into my life to come. In college I wrestled with whether to study engineering, which was a perfect fit for my mathematically wired brain, or perhaps philosophy or theology, to find a path of meaning and service in the world.

As I tried to figure this out, I was thrilled to get an internship with Senator Mark O. Hatfield after my sophomore year. It was 1976, the bicentennial summer, and the internship couldn't have been better. I learned a lot about Oregon by opening and sorting the mail each morning for the legislative correspondents who wrote the replies to the letters. I learned about tax policy when I was asked to staff the Tax Reform Act of 1976, which came up on the floor of the Senate that summer. This was before there was a television camera in the chamber, let alone email or cell phones, so my job was to follow the debate on each amendment and then meet and brief Senator Hatfield as he came out of the elevator en route to the Senate chamber to vote.

One day there was a particularly complicated vote that involved, as I can best remember, a motion to amend the amendment and then someone else's motion to table the "second degree" amendment. I was trying to explain this sequence when Senator Hatfield interrupted.

"I'm late, just tell me, up or down?" Glancing at my notes, and very unsure of the right answer, I said "up." He ran into the chamber, and I ran up the stairs to the staff gallery to watch. I had no idea if I was right or not. I pictured Hatfield voting wrong. I pictured messing up an important piece of tax policy. I pictured getting fired. The odds were fifty-fifty, but good luck was with me that day.

I dropped out of college the following January to go back to D.C. to witness the start of a new administration: President Jimmy Carter was taking office. I tried to find a job on the Hill, made it to one final interview with a congressman, but failed to get the position.

That failure opened the door to a lot of adventures. During my first few months, I waited tables evenings and weekends at Lums, a sit-down hamburger joint where an average tip was twenty-five cents and the entire staff, save for one older woman, turned over in six months. In the mornings I volunteered for a newly created environmental organization,

New Directions, working on issues related to seabed manganese nodules—and the Law of the Sea treaty—the same Law of the Sea treaty that has still not come to the Senate for ratification a generation later. It was a very cold January that year, and the Potomac froze over. So on one morning, on the way to New Directions, I got out of the bus on the Virginia side of the Potomac and walked across the river on the ice, before picking up a bus on the D.C. side.

On another morning a man walked in and offered free tickets to go to a concert for endangered species at the Kennedy Center. I was delighted to take one. President Carter was up in the President's box, and Mstislav Rostropovich played the most amazing cello concert. At the end of the concert, the emcee presented Rostropovich with a beautiful painting of a whale. The woman in front of me said to her husband, "Did he say 'endangered species'?" She then proceeded to wriggle out of her jaguar coat and fold it inside out and tuck it under her arm.

I couldn't resist the temptation to say to her, as we stood up to go, "It's hard to hide that exotic coat!"

"Yes," she acknowledged. "This is awkward. I had no idea this was a benefit for endangered species."

As the year progressed, I started working afternoons and evenings going door-to-door with the Virginia Consumer Congress. The VCC was an early practitioner of a model that later moved nationwide through the Public Interest Research Groups, or PIRGs. You were given a turf to knock door-to-door. You explained your cause to the person at each door, asked them to sign a petition, and invited them to donate to the VCC. Your wages were 30 percent of your donations. If you didn't make minimum wage, you were fired.

Our cause was a bill in the Virginia legislature to get the Virginia Electric Power Company, VEPCO, to forgo building a new nuclear power plant. VEPCO said they needed the plant to help meet peak load demand when people ran their air conditioners on hot summer days. This is not a cost-effective way to meet a peak load, since nuclear power plants are very expensive. VEPCO had a big incentive to build it, however, because as a regulated utility it would get a guaranteed return on its investment. The more VEPCO spent, the more VEPCO made, and the higher the bills were for the consumers. As an advocate for the consumers, we proposed a different solution: meters that charged more at peak load, which would encourage customers to switch some of their energy demands to other parts of the day. The meters were far less expensive and less dangerous than a nuclear plant.

In this door-to-door work, you had to figure out how to connect with many different types of people in very different neighborhoods, from poor to rich. It was great training for talking to people door-to-door twenty-one years later when I started campaigning for a seat in the Oregon House of Representatives.

One day I knocked on the door of a massive house. The lady of the house invited me in to explain our mission. She told me that her husband was the President of VEPCO, but that she didn't think she always got the full story from him.

When I was done, she pulled out her checkbook and wrote a $15 check to receive our newsletter. And there it was, on the check, the name of VEPCO's President. Back at the office we had a copy of that check blown up and posted on the wall. It was a trophy from the battlefield.

I met some curious characters knocking on doors in Arlington and Alexandria, Virginia, just across the river from the nation's capital.

One man met me at the door in his bathrobe. "Did you knock on my door earlier?" he asked. "Yes," I said. He was the first door on my turf, but no one had answered, so I tried the door again at the end of the evening.

"I had a gun aimed at your head," he said coldly. "I don't like people knocking on my door."

He seemed drunk, but when he invited me to talk some more, I walked inside. He told me all about his years in the CIA, especially his involvement in the doomed Bay of Pigs invasion, as well as Vietnam. He showed me his impressive gun collection, which he had gathered from various adventures in his career. There was even a silver ceremonial sword that he said had belonged to General Douglas MacArthur. While he was talking, I started to hear sobbing coming from the other room. What evil was going on in that house? I wondered. Little seemed impossible, given this man's stories. I was relieved when the source turned out to be his second wife and former maid. It was St. Patrick's Day and they had planned to go out for dinner, but he had drunk too much and spoiled the evening.

When he was done recounting his story, I had one question. "When you reflect on it all, how do you feel about your time in the CIA?"

"When I consider it all, the killings and such," he said, "I just can't sleep at night."

Eventually the day came when a man at a door listened to my pitch and responded that he wouldn't donate, but he wanted to hire me to sell insurance. My father always disliked the pitches from door-to-door salesmen because they were too slick. If that was what I was becoming, it was time to move on to a new adventure. I quit the next day.

I took a job as a desk clerk on Thomas Circle on 14th street in D.C. When I interviewed, it seemed like a hotel in a normal business district. When I showed up for my first shift at 6 a.m., however, I discovered that it was in the heart of D.C.'s red-light district; the pimps and ladies of the night were just finishing their work as I was starting mine.

Then, come summer, Arlington County hired me to design and operate a leadership camp for teenagers. I designed the camp on the principles I had learned from the national Boy Scouts leadership camp in Philmont, New Mexico. Each lesson went through a four-stage process called guided discovery: trial run, a lesson, applied learning, and evaluation. So let's say the lesson was on how to plan a group hike. First you tried the presentation with no guidance; then you received pointers on how to do it; then you tried it again; and then the group evaluated the strong and weak points of your effort. It was a powerful way to learn.

During the summer, with a return to college approaching, I sought the help of a guidance counselor up at Georgetown University. I explained my dilemma: that I was good at math and engineering, but I was searching for a path to do something meaningful in the world and wasn't sure that was it. His response was unhelpful: "If you like engineering, then just do it."

A plan began to take shape in my mind. I had been fascinated by the introductory courses I had taken in foreign policy and Latin American politics. I had loved my time in Ghana. How about majoring in international relations? This was a fit. So that's what I did. A lot of adventures followed. My college had a program in Italy, so I took enough Italian to qualify and went to Florence the following spring. The college had a two-week excursion at the end of the trimester to Greece, so I signed up.

From there I could get a flight to Israel for $50, so off I went to hitchhike around Israel and the West Bank: wading through Hezekiah's tunnel; climbing the snake path at Masada; staying at a kibbutz; diving into the Sea of Galilee; exploring Old Jerusalem; and snorkeling in Eilat.

It was a promising time in the Middle East. Israeli Prime Minister Menachem Begin and Egyptian President Anwar Sadat had met and agreed on the return of the Sinai to Egypt. If Israel could make peace with Egypt, then it seemed conceivable that it could make peace with each of the nations that surrounded it. There was a popular song that my sister Linda used to sing and play on the piano. It was written by an Israeli and featured the line "Let there be peace on earth, and let it begin with me." Maybe peace was possible.

Back at school I founded the International Relations Society and helped set up a speakers' series. One person who I really wanted to speak was Shirley Temple Black, the childhood movie star who had served as Ambassador to Ghana. I had heard she lived in the area, so I kept asking folks if anyone had her address or number. Finally, an executive assistant at the Bechtel International Center whispered to me that she had her number and address, but that I had to guard it carefully. I called the number and left a message with a man at the house, who I presumed was Mr. Black. No response ensued, so I recruited a friend, Katy Burdick Wilson, to go with me to her house and knock on her door. As we stood on the porch, a helicopter rose up and hovered over the house. Are you kidding me? That's one hell of a security system!

Eventually I did reach Ambassador Black on the phone, and she agreed to appear under a strict limit of no more than fifty people in the room.

People loved hearing her, and the speech was a big success except for a mistake I made while introducing her. In my introduction, I referred to her as an excellent "cultural ambassador" who had built a strong connection between America and Ghana by reaching out to participate in Ghana's art and dance and music. She wanted the audience to know, however, that she was far more than a cultural ambassador and had been immersed in addressing the challenging economic and political issues between the United States and Ghana.

As graduation approached, my journey was about to take me to Mexico and Central America, but I didn't yet know it. I thought I was headed to Asia. Through the Volunteers in Asia program I was offered a two-year position in the Philippines, where I would work evaluating the effectiveness of economic development projects in the region. This was perfect—just the sort of meaningful path I was seeking.

Then tragedy struck. At least it seemed like tragedy at the time. Dwight Clark, the Director of Volunteers in Asia, pulled me aside and handed me a letter to read. The United Nations had canceled funding for the position. There was no job in the Philippines.

I scrambled and found out about a program in Mexico sponsored by the American Friends Service Committee (AFSC), the service branch of the Quakers. For decades they had worked with local communities on summer projects: A village would plan a project, and an AFSC team, consisting of half Mexicans and half Americans, would come in to help to get it done.

It sounded great. Our team of ten headed to El Encinal, whose name roughly translates to "Oak Valley." With a population of no more than 200 people, and one small town square for public dances, El Encinal was about as humble as you could get. The town was an *ejido*, born of land reform after the Mexican Revolution. It was created as an area of communal agricultural land with families individually farming and ranching on designated plots. The families in the village who held the rights to the plots were better off than the residents who helped work the plots.

But the families that were best off were the ones where fathers and brothers were traveling seasonally to work in the United States. They weren't interested in staying in the U.S. They would go for a season, then return to live with their families in the village.

The village was isolated. Highway 16 runs across the Sierra Madre mountains, from Hermosillo in the west to Chihuahua in the east. Somewhere in the middle of those mountains there's a side road, not much more than a rocky dirt track winding through the mountains. If you negotiate that road for several hours—driving about ten miles an hour, and making all the correct choices at the unmarked places where the track diverges you'll find El Encinal. The village had a slogan: *Un Paraíso Escondido*—a hidden paradise!

There in El Encinal we took on a number of modest projects. We plastered a house for the schoolteacher, repaired the desks inside the two-room school, and improved the airplane landing strip that was used in the case of a medical emergency.

Our food was simple. Tortillas and beans or tortillas and peanut butter, with more and more hot sauce thrown in as the summer progressed. Each morning, one of the mothers would help one of us make tortillas for our team. When it was my turn, the mother rendered her judgment on my efforts: *¡zapatos!* (shoe leather!). One time, we decided to organize a day of athletic competitions for the children—our own mini Olympics, followed by a party for the village. For the party we made a huge kettle of coffee, but it was hot and almost no one drank it. We reboiled that coffee for a full week thereafter before we drank the last of it.

We had little in the way of fruits and vegetables, and no meat. Then someone in the village took pity on us and gave us a chicken. We all wanted to eat it but no one wanted to kill it. So after about a week, it was my turn to cook dinner and it seemed like time for our chicken to meet its maker. I walked to the village square and asked one of the men about the best way to kill it. He grabbed it out of my arms by the head and twirled it over his head until the body came off, landed on the ground, and ran away headless until it collapsed. He handed the head back to me and simply said, "¡como eso!"—"Like that!"

Sometimes we helped individual families with gardening or milking or ranching. One day a man and his twelve-year-old nephew invited me to help them plow and plant a field. We loaded a wooden plow with a metal tip onto a mule and set off walking into the mountains with a horse and the mule and bags of seed. They liked the horse-mule combination because the horse responded better to commands, but the mule was stronger. On a knoll there was a somewhat level plot where we could plant. This was very physical work. You had to get the tip of the plow into the ground, keep the horse and mule moving, and try to plow a straight line. At the end of each row you had to lay the plow on its side as you got the horse and mule to pivot. Before they took off again, you needed to get the plow back in the ground so it didn't just skip along the surface. I learned the meaning of the old compliment, "He can plow a straight furrow."

After I watched the nephew for a while, he insisted I give it a try. I didn't do so well. The boy told me I was having trouble getting the horse and mule moving because I wasn't yelling at them loudly enough, and angry enough, with the right curse words. He told me I had to yell *Caballo puto*, as he had done. So there I was, cursing at the horse and mule. It did seem to help, and they got a big kick out of watching my efforts.

After we plowed the field, we planted it. Beans between rows of corn. You poke a stick in the ground, drop in a seed, and close it with your foot. This was not much different from the way people have farmed in villages all over the world for thousands of years.

There wasn't any electricity in the village except for a generator used at village dances, which were held about every second or third Saturday night. On those nights the lights around the village plaza would spring to life; people would drive in from neighboring villages to join the party; and ranchero music would blare from the record player and amplifier as people filled the plaza to dance the two-step.

On every other night, the stars and moon would put on a show in the darkened village. And when we looked up at those stars, we could see a satellite, Skylab, moving through the heavens. We heard on our transistor radio that Skylab was starting to fall out of orbit, and people were worried about where it would land. NASA's plan to save it with the space shuttle hit operational snafus, so they decided to fire up its boosters and ditch it in the Indian Ocean. It came down on July 11, blowing up and scattering parts across the Indian Ocean and Western Australia.

There in our isolated ranching and farming village, where the top technologies were a Ford truck and a transistor radio, it seemed almost impossible that there was a civilization somewhere that had put a space station into the sky.

* * *

I left the rural village of El Encinal to move to the packed metropolis of New York City, where the sirens were singing day and night and you had to work to find room to walk down the street. I had a six-month internship—my first paid job in international affairs at a robust $800 per month!—to work on a variety of projects for the director of the New York branch of the Carnegie Endowment for International Peace (CEIP).

There was one perk. The CEIP had just sold its building next to the United Nations and moved to rented space in Rockefeller Center. For a few weeks, before they fully staffed up, I had an office with a window on the 53rd floor of one of the most iconic buildings on the planet. Nice digs.

The CEIP was full of scholars studying complex issues around the world. It was a great place to learn. But every now and then something would remind me of the great gap between the down-home style of my blue-collar neighborhood and the so-called sophistication of the city. One of the CEIP fellows invited us to a Saturday brunch at his house. His wife asked me if I wanted a drink, using an unfamiliar word. When I sought clarification, she thought it was hilarious. She got the attention of the room, full of scholars and executives and spouses from the CEIP and announced: "Jeff has just said the most funny thing to me. I asked him if he wanted an aperitif, and he replied, 'A pair of what?'" Everyone laughed. That wasn't sophistication; that was snobbery.

CEIP had six interns. A great group. One of them, Eric Schwartz, became a lifelong friend. His family adopted me, and I spent any number of Thanksgiving and Passover weekends with them on Long Island. At CEIP Eric and I were learning everything we could about international affairs, and Central America was in the news every day.

There was a coup in late 1979 in El Salvador in which dissident military officers ousted a military strongman, followed by a brutal repression to stop a revolution, and then a bloody civil war in which the U.S. backed the El Salvadoran government and military. In Guatemala, the military was waging a dirty war against the poor, indigenous farmers and left-leaning activists, and the battles were beginning to move into the cities. Honduras had returned to civilian rule, but neighboring Nicaragua had just undergone a leftist revolution to overthrow its dictator. The whole region was in chaos.

Nicaragua was center stage. The Sandinista rebel forces had staged a raid on the legislature in August 1978, taking 2,000 hostages, earning $500,000 in ransom, and notching a significant victory. The Organization of American States facilitated negotiations between the Somoza regime and the Sandinistas with the goal of organizing elections, but

President Somoza had no intention of allowing elections, and the negotiations failed. In July 1979, just six days after Skylab fell from the sky, the Somoza regime fell, he fled into exile, and the Sandinistas took full control.

So with all of these significant developments and the United States involved in many ways, I proposed to Eric that we travel through Central America in the spring to see for ourselves the impact of U.S. foreign policy on America's backyard. We had both been admitted to the same public policy graduate program and had the spring free following our CEIP internships.

Looking back, this sounds like a crazy plan. What were we thinking? Violence and chaos everywhere. But at the time, it seemed like a fascinating opportunity to learn a lot first-hand. We developed the details. We would meet in April in San Francisco, fly to Los Angeles, and proceed south toward Costa Rica during April and May with three rules. We would speak only Spanish to improve our language skills. We would take the cheapest buses between cities. And we would sit separately on the buses to meet people, practice Spanish, and hopefully score an invitation to a home.

Our only formal planning was to get some letters of introduction from a diplomat we had encountered from the Honduran mission to the United Nations. The letters, we thought, might get us into some interesting meetings or, if necessary, out of trouble. Ironically, Honduras was the place we would be least likely to need them.

Upon arrival in a city, one of us would sit with our soft-side suitcases while the other scouted out a pension—a cheap hotel—to sleep in. The price was right, generally less than $5 a night, but the amenities were few: no air-conditioning and sporadic hot water. A room with a ceiling fan was a big score.

Many years have passed, and both of us have gone on to be involved in international affairs in many ways. Eric launched Human Rights Watch Asia and served in senior human rights roles in both the Clinton and the Obama administrations before heading up the Humphrey School of Public Policy in Minneapolis. He is now back in Washington as president of Refugees International. But whatever else we might have done, I think both of us regard this tour through Central America as a great adventure and education.

* * *

The first phase of our trip through Mexico was uneventful compared to the chaos that awaited us in Central America. The biggest challenge was helping a bankrupt American make it to Mexico City and dealing with some bad street food that knocked me out of action for days.

Then we crossed into Guatemala where we were confronted daily with evidence of conflict and violence. We showed up at the stunning shores of Lake Atitlan, in the highlands, just a week after guerrillas had locked up some foreigners in the local jail overnight so they could lecture them about income inequality. The tourists were set free the next day, undoubtedly terrified for their lives. We wondered if the guerrillas would return while we were there. We tried to travel from there to the beautiful highland town of Hue-huetenango, but the road was shut down. We were told the army was conducting village-to-village operations to kill young men. I thought at the time it was probably just a rumor—who would do such a thing?—but it turned out that was exactly what was happening.

We shifted plans and headed east toward the capital for the weekend. On our first morning in Guatemala City, we attended Saturday morning services at the synagogue, since Eric is Jewish. After the service, everyone was heading to a memorial for the president of the Chamber of Commerce, a leader in the Jewish community, who had been assassinated that week.

As we explored Guatemala City, we ran into a young man who told us that his father was flying to Tikal and that we might be able to hitch a ride in his father's plane. Since it had been raining and the roads to Tikal were virtu-ally impassable, this was our only option to see these extra-ordinary 1,000-year-old Mayan ruins. We arranged to meet him at our pension the next day. As the hour of our meet-ing approached, Eric and I were mailing some packages of Guatemalan art and weavings back to our homes, but the line was moving slowly. We decided that Eric, who was in line in front of me, would rush back as soon as he was done to meet our new friend on time. I would follow a few minutes later after I had mailed my purchases.

That five minutes of separation resulted in vastly different experiences. Eric got back to the pension and went across the narrow street—maybe twenty-five feet wide—to buy a beer. No friend in sight. He went back across the street to the pension. Shots rang out as he stepped onto the sidewalk and he dived into the doorway of the hotel.

I came around the corner to the street and saw legs poking out from between two cars. I thought that someone had been hit by a car, and I rushed up to give first aid. The man lying on the street was riddled with bullets. His whole upper torso was torn apart. A bloody mess. I staggered back, and looked up and down the street. It was deserted and deadly quiet. I jumped inside the doors of the pension.

We were rocked by the experience. The newspaper the next day said that the victim had been a professor at San Carlos University, gunned down by right-wing militia. His crime was to teach history or social studies. He wasn't alone. According to the newspaper, dozens of professors and student leaders had been assassinated over the previous year. This was insanity.

We decided to write a letter to the newspaper to describe what we had seen and to condemn the violence. As we started writing, we realized how desperate our own situation was. What the hell were we doing there? We had no support system, and there were virtually no tourists in the country. The city was full of soldiers carrying machine guns. Writing a letter condemning the right-wing death squads—the side

in this war allied with the government and the military—
might just be signing our own death warrant.

We had to get out of there. We abandoned the letter writing, checked our maps, and pondered the fastest way out
of Guatemala. We had a choice to make: the Pan-American
Highway into El Salvador or the back road to Honduras.

*   *   *

On March 24, 1980, just days before Eric and I launched
our trip south, an assassin took the life of Archbishop Óscar
Romero as he celebrated mass in El Salvador. Romero's criticisms of the country's military dictatorship had made him a
marked man. His death plunged El Salvador from sporadic
violence into a full-blown civil war. By the time a peace
agreement was reached years later, an estimated 8,000 people
had disappeared and 80,000 had died. While we were on our
trip south, there were reports of buses being stopped on the
Pan-American Highway, followed by executions of some of
the passengers.

It didn't seem like the best idea to be on one of those buses,
so we choose the back road to Honduras.

Tegucigalpa, the capital, was poor, really poor. Honduras
ranked as one of the poorest nations in the western hemi-
sphere. On the bus, I sat next to a woman who described
herself as an *educador*. She had to repeat the word several
times before I understood the obvious: She was an educator,
a teacher. When I asked her to explain her work, she said she
had been a teacher but had lost her job. She was trying to get

her license back but was running into all kinds of difficulty. She told me, matter-of-factly, that she now had to dance for a living, which I slowly came to understand meant that she was working at a brothel to support her family. We didn't know her whole story, but this much was clear: She was hard-pressed to make a living in one of the poorest nations in the world. She, like hundreds of thousands of others, was scraping by in whatever way she could to survive. She invited us to come by and meet her family, which we did.

There in Tegucigalpa, we put our letters of introduction to work. We had a meeting with a government minister to discuss the extensive logging and deforestation in the nation. He assured us that all of the concerns were misplaced, because the root system of their trees, unlike American fir trees, survived the logging, resprouted, and regrew with minimum damage to the ecosystem. No problem at all.

We also checked out the newspaper and found out that the Miss Honduras contest was going to be held that night in a ballroom at the fanciest hotel in town. We decided to see if our letters of introduction could get us in. Eric and I did our best to make our khaki pants look clean and respectable, but we looked more the part of vagabonds than diplomats. Still, nothing ventured, nothing gained. We flashed our letters of introduction and told our most charming stories. No deal. Outside the ballroom, however, was a staircase landing with a table and a window onto the event, so we sat down and pretended we were in attendance. The problem was, we couldn't hear a thing.

The young woman turning to prostitution to support her family and the wealthy families decked out for the Miss Honduras pageant represented the massive gap between millions of impoverished, struggling Honduran families and the small circle of rich and powerful Honduran elites.

From Tegucigalpa it was on to Nicaragua, and we carried a lot of dread about crossing the border. Folks in Guatemala had told me, "You think the violence is bad here? Just wait until you get to Nicaragua. They hate Americans there, because of all the American support for their former dictator, Somoza, including all the American bombs Somoza dropped on their villages." We were increasingly nervous, but there was no way to get to Costa Rica without crossing Nicaragua.

We arrived at the Honduras-Nicaragua border, where an official demanded a special fee to allow us to cross. We refused to pay what we were certain was a bribe, so we sat there all day until sunset, when she finally allowed us to proceed. We were the last people across before the border was shut down for the night. The Nicaraguan border guards told us that all the commercial vans and buses had already left, so if we wanted to get from the border post to the nearest town, we would have to ride in the bus carrying the Nicaraguan soldiers. Our hearts sank. We had heard all these stories about how much they hated Americans, and now we were going to share a ride with the forces that had just overthrown an American-backed dictator.

But what choice was there? We got on the bus full of soldiers carrying rifles. They were not a friendly crowd. The bus proceeded through some of the thickest, lushest jungle I have ever seen. It could have been beautiful, but I was absorbed considering how this might end. I kept thinking, "This bus is going to come to a stop and they are going to stand us on the side of the road and shoot us. They'll throw us in the bushes and no one will ever have any idea what happened to us. Who in the world even knows where we are?"

By the time we arrived at the village it was dark out and raining heavily. The soldiers stopped the bus on a street and told us to get out. There was no pension in sight. In fact there were no lights that suggested any business was nearby or open. A man coming down the street carrying a kerosene lantern stopped to talk to us and invited us to his house. We were rescued! He put us up in his barn for the night, where Eric and I debated who would get the hammock.

We headed down to the Pacific coast to Corinto, then went on to León. I think it was in León that there was a section in the market dedicated to all those who had died when the town was destroyed by the American bombs. It was full of pictures and commemorations of the loved ones lost. How would I feel if I met someone from a country that had bombed my neighborhood in America, perhaps killing some of my family?

Contrary to our fears, most of the Nicaraguans we met seemed happy that we were there. They seemed to be able to draw a distinction between the American government, which had supported Somoza for decades, and individual Americans interested in their country. The Nicaraguans were excited about a future out from under the thumb of a dictator. The new government had launched a national literacy campaign and was advertising it with billboards that said—in Spanish, of course—that "literacy is the guarantor of our freedom." College students were organizing to help teach in villages. And many others were talking about the vision of resources being dedicated to health clinics, and the possibility of owning and working land that had been held by a small number of very rich landholders.

Back in the United States, there was a lot of concern that Nicaragua had been taken over by Marxists, so I asked many people I met if they were a Marxist. About half said yes. And so I asked what that meant for them and heard four answers: the chance to own land; the chance to hold elections; the chance to be free of a dictatorship; and the chance to have better schools and health clinics. I asked some if they wanted to be like Cuba, and the answer was always "absolutely not." They did tell me they hoped for help from America, because they knew that Americans had fought off a dictator—King George—to win freedom just like they had. They said they desperately needed that American help, because when the Nicaraguan elites fled after the revolution, they had taken all of the country's resources with them, from the national treasury to the livestock.

In the Nicaraguan capital of Managua we crashed a press conference held by four American congressmen. They were asked if America was going to assist Nicaragua. The congressmen responded that America would assist if the new government proceeded quickly to elections. The leadership of Nicaragua had a lot of suspicion about quickly holding elections, however, because they calculated that the elites who had exploited them for so long would have the money and knowledge to manipulate those elections.

In the end, Nicaragua didn't hold elections and America didn't provide help. In October Ronald Reagan was elected president, and eventually Ollic North was in the White House basement plotting to fund soldiers to undermine the new government. The worst is that those soldiers, the Contras, often targeted teachers and health care workers—the salt of the earth. The idea that my government was paying people to kill teachers and health care workers infuriated me.

* * *

I returned to Mexico for a second summer to work on another community project: This time, it was establishing an environmental camp halfway between Mexico City and Veracruz. This was year one of a project planned by a group of individuals who had worked for AFSC for years and then formed their own nonprofit named CEDEPAC, or the Committee for Development and Peace in Central America. The land for the camp had been acquired for a song because it was environmentally devastated. It had been overgrazed by goats, and rains had swept away all of the topsoil. It seemed like a perfect place for a camp dedicated to teaching about the environment.

Our team was 18 strong: half Americans, and half Mexicans and Central Americans. We were assisting a carpenter in building the future dorms and classrooms while also running a camp for the kids, educating them about environmental issues. The kids, of course, were running everywhere, getting in trouble and sometimes getting hurt. And the young team members were full of adolescent hormones, creating other challenges. It was exhausting, emotionally and physically. As a coleader of the camp, it was the most stressful summer of my life.

One weekend in the middle of the summer, we finally had some time to rest. We took a trip to Puebla, and two of our team members planned a hike up La Malinche, a 14,640-foot volcano named after the much-hated indigenous wife of the Spanish Conquistador Cortés. The idea of hiking up a mountain seemed to me like the perfect rest and recuperation. We drove our Kombi—slang in Spanish for a Volkswagen bus—as far up the mountain as we could get. From there we found no trail, but figured we couldn't be far off if we kept hiking upward. Eventually we did find a trail, and I dragged my heel across it to mark where we intercepted it. One woman on our team, Lisa, was not in good shape and convinced everyone that she would wait at a very nice spot until we came down and would not, under any circumstance, leave that location. In my head, I knew that it was a bad idea to leave a team member alone, but what could go wrong?

We made the summit late in the day due to our late start. When we got back to where Lisa was supposed to be, she wasn't there. The sun was setting, and we were really worried. We called out her name every few minutes as we went down the mountain. Soon we were in trees and came to a ridge where the trail diverged in two, and our two team members who had planned the hike were sure we should take the right fork. This didn't look right to me, but then again, I wasn't in charge of the hike. But I also realized that I was the person in the group who had spent the most time hiking through woods growing up, and I had the habit of looking at the forest and memorizing features to keep from getting lost. And although I didn't plan the hike, I did feel responsibility as coleader of the team, so what to do? I urged the group to take the left fork, noting we could come back to this point if it turned out that I was wrong. We proceeded, and some ten to twenty minutes later came across the mark I had put on the trail with my heel on the way up. When I saw that mark, I felt indescribable relief. Night was closing in and we hadn't found Lisa, but at least we were on the right track.

We kept calling out for Lisa all the way back down the mountain. There was still no sign of her. But when we arrived at the Kombi, there she was, resting comfortably inside. A goat herder had wandered by on the mountain, exposed himself, and terrified her. She had run and hid; he had followed. Somehow by the grace of God she had found her way back, rattled but unharmed. Lesson learned: Never leave a member of the team by him- or herself on a mountain. So much for my day of rest.

It would be almost four decades before I would find my way back to the Northern Triangle, and that visit would be triggered by my concern about the treatment of the refugee children traveling north from those nations.

* * *

After Mexico, I pursued a graduate degree in economic development and public policy, spent a summer in India, and worked at the World Bank while saving money to go back to Africa. I didn't want to do theoretical work on economic development in D.C. I wanted to work on the ground on the fundamental issues of water and food and education and health. At least that was the plan. But, I had been at the World Bank for only a few weeks when I was unexpectedly offered a Presidential Management Internship (PMI) working for the Office of the Secretary of Defense with the opportunity to work on strategic nuclear weapon policy. I wrestled with which direction to go. On the one hand, this opportunity was a 100 percent diversion from the issues of world poverty and economic development that I had been preparing to work on for years. On the other hand, the biggest threat to the planet was nuclear war and the Doomsday Clock was only a few minutes from midnight, meaning the risk of nuclear war and devastation were very real. My conscience told me to take the position.

Two years later, at the end of the internship, the Congressional Budget Office (CBO) hired me to write studies on strategic nuclear weapon systems for Congress. In the fall of 1988, I was supposed to write a study on the B-2 Stealth Bomber, analyzing its mission and its cost in the context of the entire strategic triad of bombers, land-based missiles, and submarine-launched missiles. But there was a problem. The Reagan administration and, as of January 1989, the George H. W. Bush administration were keeping the program under lock and key. The program was being kept highly classified so that it couldn't be publicly debated.

There was a reason for this. The bomber's mission was unclear and controversial, and the Department of Defense didn't want Congress to ask too many questions and potentially derail the program.

Thus, I took a six-month leave of absence to wait for the opportunity to write the B-2 study. I used that time to gut and start to rebuild a town house in the Bloomingdale neighborhood of Washington, D.C. At the end of six months, my boss called me back. Even though the B-2 classification hadn't yet changed, he couldn't grant me any more leave. It was time to fish or cut bait. I chose to cut bait. I resigned from CBO and continued to rebuild the house, a project that would take me through the early months of 1991. I redesigned the interior, put on a new roof, plumbed and wired the house, installed new windows, and pretty much rebuilt the house from scratch. A big thanks goes to my dad, who introduced me to tools and the joy of building things as I was growing up.

That house project blessed me in many ways. Just after I had started working on it in the fall of 1988, my housemate Andy invited a staff member from a homeless shelter to join one of our house dinners. I was enchanted by Andy's guest, Mary Sorteberg, who had just moved to D.C. to work as a member of the Lutheran Volunteer Corps.

Mary and I went on a date a few weeks later. I had met my soul mate. Two years later we were engaged and had scheduled our wedding for June 1991, a few months after she was to return from working for four months with Mother Teresa in Calcutta. The culture shock of coming back to the United States after working with Mother Teresa and the people dying on the streets of Calcutta, however, was too much. We canceled the wedding. Mary arranged a job at Holden Village, a Lutheran retreat center in Washington State that had no access by road and no phone connection to the outside world. As she prepared to go to Holden, I prepared to move back to Oregon. We drove my red Toyota truck across the country together with Misty, my Airedale terrier, visiting Yellowstone National Park and exploring the Badlands in South Dakota.

Back in Oregon, I was at a loss. I didn't have a job and I didn't have easily transferable skills. I wasn't a teacher or a doctor or a nurse or a lawyer or a plumber or anything else that made getting a job easy. No one wanted to hire an expert on strategic nuclear policy. Those months were hard.

I had spent every dime I had renovating the house, including maxing out my credit card. To make it worse, my beloved companion, Misty, got a staph infection and died.

I needed an income. In July, I drove back to D.C. to finish a punch list on the house and to work as a temp for three weeks to get enough money to pay my credit card bill. While I was there, I got a letter from Mary saying it was time to break up so she would have the space to figure out her life. This hit me hard. I couldn't imagine life without her. This was a low point. No job, no money, no dog, no fiancée, no soul mate.

I drove back across the country to meet Mary to say good-bye as she headed for Colorado and I headed back to Oregon. If anyone had told me that 18 years from then I would be a U.S. Senator from Oregon, I would have considered it the most preposterous prediction in the world.

Back in Portland I had started volunteering with the local affiliate of Habitat for Humanity. I loved their mission of working toward a world with a decent home in a decent community for every family. And I loved the philosophy of Millard Fuller, Habitat's cofounder. He preached the theology of the hammer: We can disagree on many things, but we can all agree to pick up a hammer and help one of God's families in need.

Habitat provided the break I needed. In October the Portland affiliate hired me as its Executive Director. This completed a life circle of sorts. After a detour through years in the nuclear policy world, I was back engaged in economic development. The affiliate was struggling. It had an annual budget of $20,000, and I had to build a fund-raising operation to pay my own salary—a whopping $18,000 per year—as well as fund the organization.

I developed and launched a number of ideas in the next several years: a Walk for Humanity, a fund-raising walk through the most troubled neighborhoods of Portland; a Habitat Volunteer Corps, modeled on the Jesuit and Lutheran Volunteer Corps, in which young folks out of college dedicate a year to simple living, direct service to the poor, and spiritual community; a Sponsor This House program for companies or individuals to fund the construction of a home; and the Habitat Home Building Center, the acquisition of a building where we could store construction materials, house volunteers, and establish offices. With the approval of the Habitat Board, we were able to secure an option on a decrepit tavern and raise grants to buy it. But we still had to rebuild it. That was accomplished when I met with Dale Baugh of Baugh Construction, which had just finished a big project at the airport. Dale agreed to coordinate donated services from his subcontractors to restore the entire building.

I also teamed up with several other organizations to launch Portland YouthBuilders, which gave gang-affected youth a chance to earn a high school degree while learning carpentry and construction by building a house. During the first week of our pilot project, one of our youth was shot dead in a drug altercation. It was a rough time in Northeast Portland, with the Bloods gang controlling the neighborhood. YouthBuilders gave some youth a positive path to escape the street.

I will always love Habitat, both for the wonderful work they do and for giving me a chance to get back on my feet. And the story worked out with Mary, also. After a couple months in Colorado, she moved back to her home city of Minneapolis to work in a hospital. We met up there in December 1991 and got engaged for the second time. We tied the knot three months later in Minneapolis at Our Savior's Lutheran Church, where her father had been a pastor. Once again, we drove west in my trusty red pickup. This time to build our life together.

In 1994 I went to work for another nonprofit, Human Solutions, to develop affordable housing. I went out to meet the mother of the first family that was moving into my project, Cedar Meadows. I asked her how she liked the place. She loved that we had put in a playground, because other places she had lived had taken them out to discourage families with kids from moving in. She also loved that we had some three- and four-bedroom apartments for larger families.

I told her I had this other idea, in which a family at a place like Cedar Meadows could save money and earn a matching grant for a down payment on a house. She said, "Oh, owning a home; that would be the light at the end of the tunnel," and she started crying. OK, I thought, let's make it happen. I called the idea the Tenant Investment Program, or TIP, and put my intern Cassandra Garrison to work to find any similar program.

She quickly found the book *Assets and the Poor: A New American Welfare Policy* by Michael Sherraden, in which Michael proposed a similar but broader approach. A low-income individual could save in an Individual Development Account (IDA), and then earn a matching grant for any of the three most powerful strategies for moving from poverty to the middle class: education, small business, and home ownership. That sounded exactly right to me. So my TIP program metamorphosed and became, as far as I'm aware, the first IDA program west of the Mississippi.

Later in 1999, when I joined the state legislature, I took the idea with me. One of my first projects was to recruit a Republican from Central Oregon, Ben Westlund, and team up to pass funding to support IDAs in Oregon. Thanks to the unique tax strategy we developed, Oregon still has one of the strongest IDA programs in the country.

At Habitat for Humanity and Human Solutions, I saw the enormous power of stabilizing families through home ownership or fair rents in a well-managed complex. The parents do better, and the children do better. What a worthy cause to fight for. But as I worked in those capacities, I also spent a fair amount of time lobbying city and state officials to build stronger programs. After I talked to officials and at times struggled to get their interest, the thought occurred that it might just be easier if I could be the one in their seat.

In addition, I could see the huge difference that good and bad policy could make. A law that allows predatory home mortgages, for example, will turn the dream of home ownership into a nightmare for millions of families. A law that stops predatory mortgages will, on the other hand, lead to stability and success for millions of families.

It was thoughts like that that led me to run for the Oregon House in 1998. And when I was fed up with the paralysis of the Oregon legislature on core issues like housing, health care, education, equality, environment, and infrastructure, those thoughts led me to consider changing tracks in 2003.

I said to Mary, "Given the paralysis at the legislature, maybe I should consider changing directions. I could make this my last session in the legislature, continue to lead a nonprofit as we raise our kids, and have a wonderful life." She liked the sound of that. "Or," I said, "I could quit my paid job and dedicate every minute to building a majority in the Oregon House that would take on those issues." Mary responded that she would back me up whichever way I wanted to go. That was a fairly amazing thing for her to say. Many a spouse would have told me that I had responsibilities and that giving up the paying job was out of the question. But not Mary. I resigned my job the next day.

Shortly thereafter, I ran to be Democratic Leader of the House and won a three-way race by a single vote. A whole new slate of officers were swept into leadership. It was an amazing team, and in two election cycles we won a majority in the House and had a fabulous legislative session in 2007.

Soon after that session, there was a battle to be fought for the U.S. Senate. I got on the battlefield when everyone said victory was out of reach. You can't win if you aren't on the battlefield. And if you are there, you have a chance to win against the odds. Thanks to the Obama wave of enthusiasm and the hard work of a great team and hundreds of volunteers across the state, we won and I was headed to the U.S. Senate.

I never conceived that my journey from Myrtle Creek to remote corners of the world, and back again to Portland would someday take me to the U.S. Senate. But meeting all of those people in all of those places was the best possible preparation.

The life of a woman selling giant tree snails in Ghana is incredibly different from a teacher-turned-"dancer" in Honduras, who is different from a single mom in Portland trying to keep her kids away from gang life. A retired CIA operative in Northern Virginia couldn't be in a world more different from a villager struggling to plow a rocky field in Mexico.

But in all of these different episodes, in all of these different places, I've seen a common thread of people pursuing opportunities and dealing with challenges, seeking joy and fulfillment, playing the hand that was dealt them while trying to make their lives a little better, or at least getting through to the next day. I've seen that common humanity we all share to find safety, hope, and a brighter future.

That's what makes serving in the U.S. Senate such a privilege: the chance to help create opportunity for everyone to thrive. And it's why, when a new administration decided to treat refugees as criminals and rip children out of their arms—to deny them our shared humanity—I went on the warpath to stop them.

EIGHT

THE MISERY TRIANGLE

WHEN I TRAVELED THROUGH CENTRAL AMERICA IN 1980, the region was wracked with violence. Civil wars were underway in Guatemala and El Salvador, and Nicaragua was trying to get on its feet after the Sandinista revolution. Honduras was quiet by comparison, but the poorest of the lot. Now, four decades later, each country is a democratic republic with elected leaders. But the countries are worse off, not better. What has gone wrong?

The answer can be summed up in four words: drugs, guns, gangs, and corruption.

The three nations of the Northern Triangle—Guatemala, Honduras, and El Salvador—have become key transit points for drugs moving to America from South America. Drug cartels that control that trafficking have found it easy to operate with little resistance from the military or police. The cartels have overcome whatever resistance they encountered either through intimidation with force or through persuasion with bribes. The dollars the drug trade brought from American customers enabled the cartels to not only buy off officials but also to purchase guns smuggled from the United States. Neither the United States nor Mexico checks closely for guns traveling south from the United States, and from Mexico it is a short trip to get the guns to the Northern Triangle.

With dollars and guns the criminal empires started reaching further into the cities and down to the streets. Gangs were reinforced by seasoned gang members deported from the United States. Salvadorans who had fled the war in El Salvador formed MS-13 in Los Angeles in the 1980s. They then grew in power in Central America following large-scale deportations from the United States in the 1990s.[1] The gangs have taken over communities block by block. Extortion of businesses became near universal. As the President of Guatemala told our congressional delegation led by Senator Tom Carper of Delaware in February 2019, "Every business in Guatemala pays extortion money."

The extortion enterprise squeezes main street businesses relentlessly. The threat to those who won't or can't pay is severe. The gangs don't threaten to throw a brick through your window or break your arm. It is more like "pay us now, or we shoot you tomorrow." Or worse: "Pay us or we will kill a member of your family or rape your daughter."

If you borrow from a gang to make extortion payments or to finance a family member's trip north, you just sink deeper into a gang's grip. This violence is a major factor driving families north. When I met Gabriela and her baby daughter, Andrea, in

McAllen, she had fled Honduras because she was marked for death if her family couldn't repay a loan, and they couldn't. When I met Elena, she told me that she had fled because she ran out of funds to pay the extortion on her beauty parlor, and the gang broke into her house and molested her 14-year-old daughter Carolina with a gun to both their heads.

President Obama's administration, responding to an influx of refugees from Central America in the summer of 2014, went to work on a strategy to reduce migration from the Northern Triangle by strengthening security, economy, and governance in the region. Obama assigned Vice President Joe Biden to lead the effort. Biden laid out the plan in a *New York Times* op-ed in January 2015:

> As we were reminded last summer when thousands of unaccompanied children showed up on our south-western border, the security and prosperity of Central America are inextricably linked with our own.
>
> The economies of El Salvador, Guatemala and Honduras remain bogged down as the rest of the Americas surge forward. Inadequate education, institutional corruption, rampant crime and a lack of investment are holding these countries back. Six million young Central Americans are to enter the labor force in the next decade. If opportunity isn't there for them, the entire Western Hemisphere will feel the consequences.
>
> Confronting these challenges requires nothing less than systemic change, which we in the United States

have a direct interest in helping to bring about. Toward that end, on Monday, President Obama will request from Congress $1 billion to help Central America's leaders make the difficult reforms and investments required to address the region's interlocking security, governance and economic challenges.[2]

Biden noted that the United States was ready to help the Northern Triangle countries "provided they took ownership of the problem," and they did. Guatemala removed officials suspected of corruption and human trafficking. Honduras signed an agreement to combat corruption with Transparency International. And El Salvador passed a law providing protection for investors. The three nations forged a plan for economic and political reforms in partnership with the Inter-American Development Bank, an "alliance for prosperity."

And thus was born the "U.S. Strategy for Central America," to support the Northern Triangle's "Alliance for Prosperity." In response to Obama's request for $1 billion in funding to kick off the program in Fiscal Year 2016, Congress approved $754 million for the first year and another $700 million the following year, while placing strict conditions on the aid related to border security, corruption, and human rights. As a result of these conditions, as well as congressional holds and budget delays, aid arrived to the region slowly. For each dollar that the U.S. put into the effort through the U.S. Strategy, the Northern Triangle countries report spending $4 to $7 through the Alliance for Prosperity.

Biden's plan was ambitious and correctly identified many of the issues the three nations faced. On security, Biden noted the need to tackle both low-level and high-level crime, stabilizing neighborhoods with community-based policing and taking out the transnational criminal networks engaged in drug smuggling and human trafficking. On governance, Biden identified improving tax collection, rooting out corruption in government contracting, and strengthening the courts. And on the economy, he proposed better protections for investors and intellectual property, and oversight to make sure international assistance is spent effectively.

As Biden left office in January 2017, he tasked Tom Carper, the senior senator from his home state of Delaware, to track and maintain the U.S. Strategy for Central America. I traveled with Senator Carper to visit the Northern Triangle states in February 2019 to review progress on the project. We were joined by Representatives Donald Norcross, Don Beyer, Lisa Blunt Rochester, and Lou Correa.

I was struck by the enormity of the challenges. Income and wealth inequality are massive. Unemployment and malnutrition are high. Fierce gangs routinely extort funds from Main Street businesses, sapping their vigor and channeling funds upward to the cartels. Schools and health clinics are inadequate. Corruption among the elite power brokers, who have operated outside the reach of the law for generations, is extensive. Domestic violence is epidemic. Guatemalans have a saying that captures the plight of the region: We are too far from God and too close to the United States of America.

One set of pictures from Guatemala sticks in my mind. John Beed, the Guatemala Mission Director of the U.S. Agency for International Development, showed our congressional delegation one picture of nine-year-old Guatemalan children raised in Guatemala, and a second picture of nine-year-old Guatemalans raised in the United States. In both pictures, lines on the wall behind the children marked different heights so you could tell how tall the children were. The children raised in Guatemala were six inches shorter than the group raised in America. Limited calories and nutritional deficiencies have produced extensive stunting throughout the Northern Triangle.

Another factor that drew our attention was the murder rates. In 2015, when a truce between the MS-13 and the 18th Street gangs collapsed, murders in El Salvador soared. The murder rate hit 105 people per 100,000, which was the highest in the world for a nation not at war.[3] President Sánchez Cerén responded by writing a new chapter in *mano dura*—the iron fist—giving police the ability to use force without fear of suffering consequences; and in 2016 the legislature supported the creation of elite police units with extensive powers to conduct searches and seizures.

The effectiveness of the *mano dura* strategy is much debated. Murder rates have dropped across the Northern Triangle, but this may have more to do with a periodic truce between the major gangs than with *mano dura*. Some analysts believe that *mano dura* has made crime worse, not better. Gang leaders have used prison time to organize and strengthen their operations, and the crackdown may have driven more young people to join the gangs.[4] Meanwhile, murder rates remain very high on a world scale. Comparing 2014 to 2018, the murder rate in Guatemala dropped from 31 to 22.4, and in Honduras from 66 to 40. And in El Salvador, after the peak in 2015 of 104, the rate dropped to 68.6 in 2018. For comparison, the murder rate in the United States is about 5. Whatever the effect of *mano dura* is on murder rates, human rights and due process are casualties.

During our trip, I kept asking for examples of anywhere that people had succeeded in taking their communities back from the gangs. I received one answer: San José Guayabal in El Salvador. Mayor Mauricio Vilanova patrols the streets of his community of 13,000 wearing a bulletproof vest and armed with a Galil SAR assault rifle.[5] MS-13 and the 18th Street gangs came to the town in 2006. Citizen patrols helped push them out, but they returned in 2012, taking advantage of a truce with the government to expand their territory. Vilanova revived his patrols accompanied by town hall officials. He has built a network of 300 informants to spot renewed gang activity, invested in security cameras, assigned mentors to at-risk youth, and built up education and sports as an alternative to the gangs. The number of murders in his town in 2018? Zero.

The mayor's approach is not without critics who observe his vigilante style. But there is a lot to learn from his efforts. The whole community is involved, and the whole community benefits. Carmen Garcia, a grandmother, told a reporter

"We feel free. The children can play."[6] If the Northern Triangle countries are going to break the grip of the gangs, every successful effort like San José Guayabal merits close study.

Another challenge in the region is relatively high birth rates, which generate a large number of young people reaching the job market each year in economies that generate few jobs. Guatemala's birth rate is almost twice that of the United States, at 24 births per 1,000 people compared to 12.5 in the U.S.

Poverty and the shortage of jobs are economic drivers for migration to the United States. But there is another driver as well: ambition. In El Salvador we heard that in rural villages you will see shack after shack after shack and then a modern well-built home. That home is paid for by remittances—money sent home from the United States—from a family member who has found work in America. These homes become a powerful advertisement for young men and women to head north. The remittances make up a good share of the GDP of the Northern Triangle nations. In 2017 they constituted 11.2 percent of Guatemala's GDP, 18.8 percent of Honduras' GDP, and 20.4 percent of El Salvador's GDP. The economies of these nations would collapse without remittances. Remittances to the three nations together hit almost $16 billion in 2017 and more than $17 billion in 2018. This swamps the resources that the United States has invested in the U.S. Strategy for Central America.

As Senator Carper's congressional delegation visited each of the Northern Triangle nations, we asked for a detailed briefing on expenditures from the U.S. Strategy for Central America and the corresponding efforts of each nation under the Alliance for Prosperity. In each nation we are supporting roughly a dozen programs in each of the three categories: promoting prosperity, enhancing security, and improving governance. It's a dazzling array of projects. I came away with two key questions: How do we evaluate the effectiveness of each? And would it make more sense to focus on a smaller number of programs that have the biggest impact?

In each nation I asked the President what the most effective program was. I got a clear answer from President Jimmy Morales of Guatemala: "School lunch programs help the most," he said. "They are one of the most powerful things you can do because it helps keep kids in school and helps address malnutrition. You also create some jobs in a village and teach some mothers how to cook better food at home."

Answers from the presidents of Honduras and El Salvador were far more general. But I was heartened to hear USAID in El Salvador state that they were going through a rigorous analysis to see which programs work best. They want to know not only what best improves the economy or public health or public safety, but also the impact on migration.

*   *   *

In each nation, we spent a lot of time discussing the challenge of corruption. The campaign against corruption has taken a different form in each of the three countries of the Northern Triangle. Guatemala struck a deal establishing the

UN International Commission Against Impunity in Guatemala, commonly known by its Spanish initials, CICIG. CICIG, under the leadership of Iván Velásquez, a Colombian prosecutor, has taken a very public role in attacking corruption as it provided extensive investigative support to the Guatemalan Public Ministry, an equivalent to the U.S. Department of Justice. Honduras established the Mission to Support the Fight Against Corruption and Impunity in Honduras (MACCIH), which played a very similar role to CICIG but operated more discreetly. And in El Salvador, international assistance directly supported the corruption-fighting power of the Attorney General's office.

"Impunity" is an interesting word. It is not a word that we use much in the United States. In the Northern Triangle, however, one encounters it everywhere. It describes the conduct of the powerful elites who for generations have operated without fear of being prosecuted for breaking the law. This corruption has multiplied the wealth of those elites while sustaining the desperate poverty of the rest of the citizens. And that is exactly why the campaign against impunity is central to improving the economic prospects of ordinary people in Central America. If those prospects don't improve, thousands of Central Americans will keep fleeing north.

Tackling corruption is not an easy task. Once the campaign starts to become effective, the powerful elites respond by working to undermine it. This has been particularly evident in Guatemala. President Jimmy Morales—an outlandish TV star turned political newcomer who ran against a former first lady—won his office in 2015 campaigning on corruption. His slogan was *"Ni corrupto ni ladrón"*—Neither corrupt, nor a thief.

If he were serious about taking on corruption, he had a powerful partner in CICIG. Backed by the UN, CICIG hired international prosecutors and brought in powerful investigative tools, including wiretapping, to support Guatemala's Attorney General and Public Ministry. With this support, the attorney general's office produced impressive results, prosecuting dozens of high-ranking officials and businessmen. Guatemala's previous president, Otto Pérez Molina, was forced out of office by corruption charges and now sits in prison. Molina's predecessor, Alvaro Colom, was also imprisoned on corruption charges until he was released on bail in August 2018.

But since taking power, Morales has worked to undermine CICIG as its investigations have targeted many in top business and political circles. He was very upset when CICIG prosecutors started looking into graft by his son and his brother in 2016, and none too pleased when Velásquez, the CICIG Commissioner, announced in 2017 that President Morales could not account for nearly a million dollars of campaign funding. Morales responded by declaring Velásquez "persona non grata" and ordering him to be expelled from the country. The Guatemalan courts stepped in to defend CICIG, but President Morales continued to work to undermine its authority, announcing that he won't renew CICIG's mandate when it expires in September 2019.

The Guatemalan Congress got into the act, voting to

protect Morales from further investigation. They also passed an "impunity pact" to protect themselves from prosecutions for graft, but the public outcry on this was fierce and the Congress reversed itself.

Morales and powerful business and political leaders have developed a broad campaign to undermine CICIG and the Public Ministry at home and in the United States. Morales argued passionately to our congressional delegation that CICIG is damaging the economy and hurting all Guatemalans by bringing corruption charges against the business community, making companies afraid to make deals and civil servants afraid to sign documents. He declared that he wanted to see CICIG investigated for the damage it has done to the economy and his country.

Leaders across civil society told our delegation how misguided this was. They contended that anti-corruption investigations were not hurting the economy. It is the other way around: One cannot improve the economy without taking on corruption first.

Morales and the power elite also paint CICIG's work as an attack on Guatemala's sovereignty, contending that CICIG is an international scheme to take over the judicial system in Guatemala. The flaw in this argument is that CICIG's only power is to provide support and advice to Guatemala's Attorney General, who ultimately makes the decisions about investigations and prosecutions. Guatemala's sovereignty is fully intact.

Another strategy opponents use is to portray CICIG as

subservient to Russia and president Putin because it investigated and charged a Russian oligarch who is a critic of Putin. Igor Bitkov and his family settled in Guatemala but were caught up in an investigation of corruption in the migration agency when the investigators discovered that Bitkov had bought fake Guatemalan passports for $50,000 apiece for his family.

Perhaps the most disturbing part of the campaign against CICIG is a plan spawned in February 2017, when a group of Guatemalan business and political leaders gathered in a condominium in Guatemala City to develop a plan to derail CICIG that included hiring lobbyists in the United States. They hired two firms, Barnes & Thornburg in Indiana, which has close ties to Vice President Pence, and Greenberg Traurig in Florida, which has close ties to members of Congress and top executives in the Trump administration. They paid each $80,000 per month.[7]

It is hard to know just how each of these elements has played into a change in U.S. policy, but the formerly strong bipartisan support for CICIG has definitely eroded. In March 2018, Nikki Haley, then U.S. Ambassador to the United Nations, reportedly joined Kevin Moley, the U.S. Assistant Secretary of State in the Bureau of International Organization Affairs, in advocating within the administration for cutting off U.S. funding for CICIG.[8]

And two months later, Senator Marco Rubio announced he was placing a hold on $6 million in funding for CICIG.[9] He disclosed that he was concerned that CICIG "has been manipulated and used by radical elements and Russia's campaign against the Bitkov family in Guatemala." Senators Roger Wicker and Mike Lee, along with Representative Christopher Smith of New Jersey, joined Rubio in a letter addressed to the foreign relations committees of both the House and Senate asking for funding for CICIG to be suspended.

The future of the fight against corruption in Guatemala, Honduras, and El Salvador will depend on the outcome of future elections in each country and on the future of U.S. support for anti-corruption efforts. As Guatemala has made clear, the powerful in the Northern Triangle will use every tool in the book to escape accountability and maintain their ability to operate outside the reach of the law.

As we consider the challenges the governments face in the Northern Triangle and how the U.S. might help them reclaim control of their countries from the gangs and the drug cartels, we are going to have to conduct a very intensive examination of what is working and what isn't, and decide whether the U.S. should make a much more robust effort to assist them.

Even as I write these words, President Trump is arguing that the U.S. should cut funding to the U.S. Strategy for Central America to persuade the Northern Triangle governments to stop the flow of migrants north. This is not going to work. The governments are too weak to implement aggressive measures to stop citizens from migrating. And cutting the modest support we provide would only make the situation on the ground worse for ordinary people, making migration more likely. We will have to come up with a better plan.

NINE

BORDER BLOCKADE

I MET A BEAUTIFUL BABY GIRL NAMED ANDREA ON FATHER'S Day, 2018, and forever more she will symbolize in my mind Trump's strategy of blocking migrants at the ports of entry and leaving them stranded across the border. I met her when I returned to McAllen two Sundays after my first trip, this time with congressional reinforcements.

On this trip we were accompanied by a huge pack of media reporters, as compared to coverage from a handful of local affiliates and newspapers on the first trip. There were cameras at the airport and media tents at the border. There was Gayle King from CBS News, MSNBC reporters and anchors, and magazine reporters from *Esquire* and *Rolling Stone*.

Given the heightened public interest, U.S. officials had worked overtime to push their problems out of sight. The CBP processing center that we saw jammed with people two weeks earlier was now near empty. The freezing holding cells nicknamed *las hieleras*? Almost empty.

And what about the migrants who were stranded on the Hidalgo-Reynosa Bridge in the burning summer heat two weeks earlier? I was really interested in checking that out, since I had missed it on my first trip because of the delayed flight from Houston.

As we approached the bridge, a CBP officer told us, "There's nothing to see."

"Well, two weeks ago there were fifty or so migrants on the bridge," I said. "We're going out on the bridge to look for ourselves."

"If you cross the center line on the bridge, you're going to have to go through an official process to come back in," he warned us.

"Really?" I asked.

"Yeah," he said matter-of-factly. "You'll lose an hour. We'll have to process you coming back in."

We had heard that there were Mexican guards on the other end of the bridge who were working in cooperation with the CBP to make it harder for migrants to reach the border line on the bridge to present themselves for asylum. I wanted to go over and talk to those Mexican guards and see what they were doing, but the CBP officials obviously didn't want that to happen.

We went out to the middle of the bridge anyway, and sure enough the bridge was empty. But there was something worse: American CBP officers were stationed in the middle to stop any migrants who got past the Mexican officers from taking a step across the line into America, since with that step they would be eligible to ask for asylum. Obstructing someone from asking for asylum is, in the view of many legal experts, a violation of national and international law. But there it was, happening right in front of us.

We returned to the port of entry building at the base of the bridge. I asked the CBP officer why they were blocking migrants from coming across to ask for asylum, especially since this is a right guaranteed by international and national law.

"We're just so overwhelmed with people," the officer said.

"It's not very crowded in here," I said. "How are you overwhelmed?"

"Well we have staff shortages," he explained. "It's the whole pipeline. We're backed up all the way."

I asked if they had allowed any migrants to cross the bridge that day, and he indicated that they had allowed a few across.

The system didn't look overwhelmed at that moment. The interview rooms were empty. And the processing center that we had visited earlier was thinly populated. But there was one room at the port of entry building with ten or twelve people in it, so I asked if there was anyone in there who did not have a passport or visa. Was there a family seeking asylum? He said yes, there was one. Could we talk with that family? He said he would bring them out.

And that is how we met Andrea, a beautiful little girl, just sixty-five days old, cradled in her mother's arms. Her mom, Gabriela, told us that her family had taken a loan from a private bank—which I took to mean a street gang or a drug cartel—and that if the family couldn't pay back the loan she was the one they had targeted to die. The family had no funds to pay back the loan, but she didn't think they would kill her while she was pregnant. So with one month left of her pregnancy, she fled for her life. After a month on the road, she gave birth. It took her two more months to make it to the border.

"Did the guards let you pass because you have your child in your arms? Did they make an exception for you?" I asked her. Our translator assisted us with her comments.

"No," she said, downbeat about her situation. "I was rebuffed three times trying to cross."

"Well then, how did you get here?"

Her face just lit up at my question. She had beat the American blockade and had a moment of joy about that.

"It was too dangerous to stay on the Mexican side, so after being rejected so many times I thought: What can I do? I saw there were two bridges: there was the pedestrian bridge and the car bridge. And on the car bridge there were people washing windows for tips. So I went and asked to borrow a squeegee from one of the window washers; and I washed windows from one car to the next until I was on the American side."

I asked Gabriela what had happened with the bank loan. She said that because she had fled, and because the family couldn't repay the loan, "they killed my uncle."

Gabriela had made it into America, but her challenges

were far from over. I found out later that because she had crossed the car bridge, the CBP officials treated her as if she had crossed between ports of entry. She was taken to the processing center, then eventually fitted with an ankle bracelet and released. I picture her finding her way to a respite center like the Sacred Heart center I visited on my first trip to McAllen.

What we were witnessing that day, as well as the blockade that left families stuck on the bridge two weeks earlier, was the early phase of "metering." This is the strategy of letting only a few migrants a day cross the border at ports of entry, and leaving the rest stranded in Mexico.

By metering—blocking access at the middle of the bridge the U.S. government was exposing the migrants to harm and persecution by gangs on the Mexican side of the border. Refugees are easy targets for exploitation because they don't have friends and family nearby to provide protection, and their vulnerability is increased when they have to live on the streets because they don't have funds for a hotel and can't find space in a shelter. Assaults and rape are common. And it is not unheard of for a gang to kidnap refugees and hold them for ransom extorted from relatives in the United States.

* * *

After hearing about the many obstacles to reaching the U.S. from Mexico and the conditions they had to endure, I needed to see it for myself. So in March 2019 I went with Congressman Lou Correa to Tijuana. There are about 30 small shelters in Tijuana assisting migrants. Some are for children; others for families; and one for LGBTQ migrants who are an extremely vulnerable group in Central America. We visited seven of them. We also went to the border crossing to witness first-hand what migrants had to go through to get to America.

"Una Luz de Esperanza." A Light of Hope. That is the name of the family shelter we visited in Benito Juarez, a dusty, working-class neighborhood in Tijuana. The name of the shelter describes not only the shelter's mission, but also the energized force of its founder, Leticia "Leti" Herrera. Each day she takes in as many families as possible to protect them from the dangers of the street as they await an opportunity to seek asylum in the United States. I asked Leti how she became motivated to establish this shelter. She told me that years ago her son died from a tragic accident. She was deeply depressed for a long time. Then one day she said to herself, "You have to do something useful with the balance of this life you've been given." And she went to work helping others.

As she gave us a tour, I was amazed how many families she has been able to accommodate on the property. One room, the size of a modest conference room, was hosting seventeen families. There were four sets of bunk beds for a total of eight, plus another nine mattresses on the floor, one family to a mattress. Other rooms were similarly packed. And outside small tents were pitched between the property line and the building. Each day, a small group of women at the shelter are assigned to cook for all. The mood is more upbeat than you would imagine. Families are finding support in their common predicament. They share information and stories. They keep the place clean. Children are playing outside, laughing and sliding down the concrete side of the staircase.

*   *   *

On Sunday morning, March 17, 2019, Congressman Correa and I got up early to witness the border blockade that was leaving so many desperate refugees stranded in Mexico. We went to an open plaza at the Mexican side of the border crossing in Tijuana, called El Chaparral. A table was set up under an 8′ by 8′ canopy, and we were told that at some point the keepers of the "book" would appear and start reading names out of it. The book is a large bound registry in which names of refugees are recorded in the order of their arrival.

As we stood on the square, the keepers of the book arrived and placed it on the table. An anxious crowd gathered, hoping that their names would be called. If a person's name was called, he or she would have the chance to travel to the American side of the border to have a "credible fear" interview with an immigration judge. If the refugee described circumstances to the judge that matched the conditions for qualifying for asylum, then the refugee would have the opportunity for an asylum interview in the future.

One of the book keepers started calling out names. After a name was called, there would sometimes be an uncomfortable silence because some refugee wasn't there and had missed his or her opportunity. When other names were called, we would hear a jubilant "Si!" as a member of the crowd came forward to have his or her identification checked against the book. If it matched, the refugee was sent to line up along a fence. Earlier that morning a CBP officer had called a book keeper to say that CBP had 35 spaces available for interviews. The book keepers called out names until each position was filled.

We walked across the square and up the ramp at the start of the walkway that leads from El Chaparral on the Mexican side of the border to San Ysidro on the American side. As we crossed the plaza to the ramp, we walked past uniformed Mexican officers and what appeared to be private security guards who checked refugees approaching the pedestrian crossing in order to turn back those who had no visas or passports. It is particularly hard for a child to make it past these guards, since a child stands out from the adults who are crossing for business or tourism.

From our elevated perch we could look down into a yard where the refugees who had been called out were loaded into vans. Instead of simply walking this group up the walkway to America, the Mexican agents bused them to another point of passage a short distance away, perhaps to separate them from the chaos of the refugees filling the square in El Chaparral.

Congressman Correa and I walked back down into the square. Newly arriving immigrants were forming a line to get their names added to the book. The individuals whose names we heard called out that Sunday morning had lined up to have their names recorded into the book on February 7, 38 days earlier. But the backlog of waiting refugees was getting longer. With a wait list of over 3,000 refugees, and an average of only 40 credible fear interviews a day, the newly arriving refugees could be waiting far more than 38 days.

Who are the book keepers? The Mexican government says the book is kept by the refugees themselves. Immigration advocates say that in reality, the Tijuana book is kept by individuals supervised by Grupo Beta, a branch of the Mexican immigration service. The story that the book is managed by refugees seems to be a way for both the American and Mexican governments to sidestep responsibility.

Many Americans don't want to believe that metering is real, that our government is actually turning away refugees seeking asylum at the border. Metering brings to mind the notorious case from 1939, when the United States turned away the German ocean liner *St. Louis* at the port of Miami, forcing it to return to Europe. The 937 passengers were mostly Jewish refugees; more than a quarter of them died in the Holocaust.[1]

It has been 80 years since America turned away the *St. Louis*. Are we once again turning away refugees and leaving them stranded in dangerous circumstances? To answer this question and other issues related to child separation, the DHS Inspector General conducted surprise visits to CBP and ICE facilities at El Paso and McAllen, Texas, on June 26 to 28, 2018. His conclusion, in the formal words of an investigator: "DHS regulated the number of asylum-seekers entering the country through ports of entry at the same time that it encouraged asylum-seekers to come to the ports."[2]

The metering system is open to all kinds of scandal. The book keepers in Tijuana seemed to be operating straight up, recording names on a first-come, first-serve basis. I asked refugees in several shelters if they had had to pay a fee to get in the book or stay in the book. They all said no. But at many other ports of entry there are reports of corruption regarding management of the book. A report by ACLU found that since late 2018, "staff began to document cases of extortion of migrants by Mexican immigration agents at the Brownsville ports of entry. Agents continue to charge migrants upwards of $300 USD for access to 'metering' lists established at CBP's request."[3] At another port, immigration advocates are sure the list is controlled by the local drug cartel, which extorts fees from the refugees.

The metering system should not exist at all. But as long as the Trump administration keeps it in place, is there really any reason that the U.S. and Mexican governments can't work out a plan to have this system regulated so that it is not one more point at which refugees are exploited?

* * *

However difficult it is for adult refugees in Tijuana, it is worse for the children. Adults can register in the book at El Chaparral. Children can't. This really leaves the children in a fix. The streets of Tijuana and other border cities are extremely dangerous. There are gangs that are ready to exploit vulnerable children, including assaults, rapes, kidnapping, and extortion. There are others who will try to pull the children into the rampant child sex industry in Tijuana and other border cities.

The children can keep trying to get across the border at the port of entry, but that requires slipping past the Mexican guards. And if they succeed in that, they still have to get past the U.S. CBP officers who are prepared to block them from stepping across the border line.

Al Otro Lado—a nonprofit that assists migrant children with legal help in requesting asylum—tried to escort three boys across the border in Tijuana on March 21, 2019.[4] They dressed up the boys to make them look like middle-class tourists rather than ragamuffin refugees. They made it past the Mexican guards and got to the gate at the border line, but the CBP officers wouldn't let them cross, saying that they needed to summon a supervisor. Ten minutes later, a Mexican security officer arrived and told them they had to leave and go back into Mexico, and the U.S. CBP officer told them that since they were still standing on Mexican territory, they had to obey. The boys held on until more Mexican border officers arrived and threatened to call in the Mexican police. The boys had been there for an hour, but in fear of arrest and deportation, gave up and returned to a shelter in Tijuana.

Nicole Ramos, an attorney who works for Al Otro Lado, summed up the situation like this: "These children are incredibly psychologically damaged from being forced to wait for months in Tijuana and are growing desperate. Many discuss throwing themselves over the wall. It should not be that children must risk their lives because the adults in two governments cannot find it within themselves to act in accordance with federal and international law recognizing the rights of these children to migrate in search of protection."[5]

If the children can't cross at the port of entry, they have three options, all flawed. They can try to hang out at a shelter in Mexico that will provide community and safety, but that leaves them in a perpetual state of limbo. I met children at the Tijuana shelters who had been there for months. In addition, the streets outside the shelters remain dangerous. In December 2018, three boys from a shelter were approached by a young woman looking for a lost dog. Later, offering sex, she lured them into a room where they were attacked by her associates. Two were strangled and stabbed to death. The third escaped by promising to go for money.[6]

A second option is for the children to turn themselves over to DIF (Desarrollo Integral de la Familia), the Mexican child protection agency. DIF might offer some asylum in Mexico, but in most cases DIF will lock up the children and deport them back to Central America to the persecution they fled initially.

The third option is to cross the border between ports of entry. This can involve a lot of additional risk, but to children stranded indefinitely in Mexico, it can seem like a risk worth taking. President Trump often says that migrants should come to the ports of entry rather than crossing between them, but Trump's border blockade induces exactly the opposite behavior.

* * *

When I was in Tijuana, I was told by an official of our government that CBP was changing its policy, and that children would be allowed to approach the border, cross it, and ask for asylum. But after that I heard reports that children were still being turned away, so I arranged a phone conversation with Pete Flores, CBP Director of the San Diego Sector, and Sidney K. Aki, CBP Director of the San Ysidro Port. They both denied that children are turned away at the border. In fact, they said that CBP had a policy that CBP officers are to facilitate the passage of children who present themselves at the border.

I shared what the immigration advocates had told me about children being turned away, even when they were escorted by volunteers. They said, again, that this was not their policy. Aki told me, "We treat the children similar to how we treat our own families. We move as quickly as possible."

I asked if trainings were held so that the CBP officers at the border crossing knew that they were to assist children across the border line when children present themselves. They assured me that such trainings, called "musters," were held. I asked if there was a written policy. They said there was. I asked for a copy, and the Congressional Liaison for CBP chimed in to say she would have it in my hands the following day, Friday, April 5, 2019.

I asked for a written copy of the policy so that if there was one, I could encourage improved training for CBP officers, because clearly some of them were obstructing children at the border line, not helping them. And if the policy had loop-holes or was unclear, I could press for an improved policy. In my heart, I suspected either the policy or the trainings were not as clear and thorough as Flores and Aki described, but I hoped I was wrong, because leaving children stranded on the Mexican side of the border is a terribly cruel thing to do, and I would expect and hope far better of our government.

The next day came and went: no document. I urged my staff member, Matt Traylor, to stay in close touch with the CBP Congressional Liaison. I wanted her to know that we weren't just going to forget about this in the rush of an intense congressional schedule. The official response came on Monday: "I was informed by our office of chief counsel that CBP never shares muster documents outside the agency. I was unaware of this, or I would have stepped in on the call." This is unacceptable. Congress cannot exercise oversight if basic policy documents are hidden from them.

Al Otro Lado was not the only organization bearing wit-ness to the treatment of children at the border. The ACLU issued a report on the Texas border that found that "Despite local CBP leadership's guarantee that particularly vulnerable populations would not be subjected to the 'metering' policy, ACLU volunteers documented numerous cases of pregnant women, Mexican asylum seekers, and unaccompanied chil-dren rejected by CBP officers at ports in both El Paso and the Rio Grande Valley sectors."[7]

When CBP was asked about the children turned away at the border, a CBP spokesperson responded: "CBP processes all unaccompanied alien children who present themselves at and between the ports of entry and prioritizes their immediate intake and other vulnerable populations. The health and welfare of children at our borders is of utmost importance and their safety is of paramount concern while in our custody."[8]

I like those sentiments. CBP "prioritizes their immediate intake." And "the health and welfare of children at our borders is of utmost importance." But words aren't what matters. Actions matter. And our government under Trump's direction is deliberately leaving children stranded in hostile, dangerous territory. This is wrong. This is evil. And we must all fight to publicize it, pressure our government, and change it.

*   *   *

The UN Universal Declaration of Human Rights establishes the right to seek asylum from persecution. The 1951 Refugee Convention provides details, establishing that a person can seek asylum based on a legitimate fear of persecution in their home country on the grounds of race, caste, nationality, religion, political opinions, or participation in a particular social group. U.S. federal law also recognizes the right to asylum, observing that a person has the right to ask for asylum within one year of arriving on U.S. soil and that the granting of asylum is dependent on the refugee establishing "that race, religion, nationality, membership in a particular social group, or political opinion was or will be at least one central reason for persecuting the applicant."[9]

But President Trump and his team have been working to

curtail this right. On November 9, 2018, the Trump administration issued a regulation making anyone who crosses the U.S. border between ports of entry ineligible to apply for asylum. This contradicts a provision of federal law that permits individuals to apply for asylum either at or between ports of entry. There was a particular reason that Congress put this provision in the law. Congress wanted to give Border Patrol agents the power to quickly deport people they apprehend between ports of entry without the protection of a court hearing, but at the same time it wanted to make sure that the U.S. didn't break international and national law by deporting individuals quickly back into the hands of those who are persecuting them. The solution was to make it clear that individuals fleeing persecution could seek asylum between ports of entry as well as at ports of entry.

The administration argues that its regulation is appropriate because it encourages people to seek asylum in an orderly manner at ports of entry. But that is a cynical argument, since the administration is simultaneously blocking people from seeking asylum at the ports of entry.

Trump's new regulation was challenged on the grounds it violates existing law, and U.S. District Court Judge Jon S. Tigar issued a temporary restraining order halting implementation of the policy. An appeal is pending.

*　*　*

Another way the Trump administration has devised to deliberately harm migrant families is the Migrant Protection Protocols (MPP), also known as the "Remain in Mexico" policy. Under MPP policy, migrants from Central America who pass an initial "credible fear" interview are returned to Mexico to await an asylum hearing roughly forty-five days later. As with the "book," this places migrants at great risk, alone and without a support network, in a city where gangs, murders, and trafficking present constant dangers.

By mid-March 2019, several hundred migrants who had passed the first phase of the asylum process, the credible fear test, had been returned to Tijuana under the MPP program to await a notice for their asylum hearing. The first asylum hearings under the MPP program were scheduled for March 14 for three migrants. It was a comedy of errors. ICE scheduled the hearing for the nineteenth, then accidentally moved it to the fourteenth, then moved it back to the nineteenth, and then kept it on the fourteenth. Two of the three migrants scheduled didn't make it because of the changes.

A woman from Honduras heard at the last minute about her hearing time being moved and missed by an hour her 9:00 a.m. meeting with CBP officials, who were to take her to San Diego. Jason Aguilar, chief counsel for ICE, moved for her to be deported. One problem: She wasn't in the United States. Assistant Chief Immigration Judge Rico Bartolomei rescheduled her hearing.

The second potential hearing was for a Honduran man who didn't show up because he didn't get word about the schedule change. Aguilar again recommended deportation. But again, as with the migrant scheduled for the first hearing, he wasn't in the United States. Bartolomei rescheduled his hearing for the nineteenth. But there was another problem: The judge didn't have an address to send the hearing notice to. He asked ICE to deliver it.

Another man from Honduras was scheduled for the third asylum hearing. Although he was the only one who didn't have an attorney, he did show up. Judge Bartolomei asked if he would like another month to prepare for the hearing. "Yes," the man replied. The judge rescheduled the hearing but then added that he knew the man would still have a difficult time getting legal help while staying in Mexico.[10]

The MPP has many problems. It places the migrants in an incredibly dangerous position to spend an additional forty-five days across the border without friends, family, or resources. It is very difficult for migrants living on the street or in a shelter to find an attorney or to prepare for an asylum hearing on their own. In addition, communication regarding hearing times and procedures are difficult when the migrants don't have a permanent address or a phone.

On top of all that, the Trump administration based MPP on a twisted reading of immigration law. The law appears to convey that migrants "from" Mexico—meaning Mexicans—can be returned to Mexico to await an asylum hearing. However the Trump administration decided not to apply the law to Mexicans, but instead to apply it to migrants from Central America since they were arriving "from" Mexico by traveling "through" Mexico. On April 8, 2019, U.S. District Judge Richard Seeborg issued a nationwide preliminary injunction that blocks the MPP program. He ruled that forcing migrants back into Mexico, "where they face undue risk to their lives and freedom," violated both U.S. laws and the 1952 Refugee Convention.[11] Four days later, the Ninth Circuit temporarily halted Judge Seeborg's order and allowed DHS to implement the MPP policy while litigation continues.

Robert Moore covered the stories shared by refugees at subsequent MPP hearings for The Texas Monthly.[12] Two fathers told Immigration Judge Nathan Herbert that the day before their hearing, they were kidnapped at gunpoint after leaving a church shelter in Ciudad Juarez, held for three hours, beaten and robbed. They broke one of the men's fingers and took the last money he had: five pesos worth about 25 cents. A mother told the judge about how she had stepped out of a shelter and a man tried to kidnap her son. A number of refugees conveyed their fear that they would have nowhere to sleep when they were returned to Mexico after the hearing because the demand for shelter space was so high. Others noted that it had been impossible to arrange legal assistance because they were only allowed "two three-minute calls per week." Others explained that their 16-day Mexican tourist visas were about to expire, putting them at risk of deportation. The Legal Coordinator for Annunciation House in El Paso, Taylor Levy, assisted families at the MPP hearings. She expressed the challenge of speaking to families about their cases: "So much of what they wanted to talk about is, 'Don't you understand? I have nowhere to sleep tomorrow night, and I'm in danger.'"

Trump's border blockade may well end up rivaling his child separation policy for the amount of trauma it inflicts on refugees.

TEN

RELIGHT LADY LIBERTY'S TORCH

AS I PONDER AMERICA'S TREATMENT OF REFUGEES, I'M reminded of those grainy black-and-white videos and photos of immigrants arriving by the boatload in New York harbor over a century ago. People are lining the ship railings waving or doffing their hats to the Statue of Liberty.

I wonder what those people would think about our government's current policies toward migrants, and especially toward children. What would they make of child separation? Or of border blockades leaving refugee children and adults stranded in Mexico? Or of prisons designed to hold thousands of migrant children at one time? Or of national leaders characterizing migrants as rapists and murderers or dehumanizing them with words like "animals" and "infestations"?

President Trump has taken America to a dark place. A place deeply rooted in racism. A place deeply connected to a political strategy based on dividing America into groups and pitting one group against another.

This is doing great damage to our national soul. And we need to end it. Instead of division, we need to stand together. We need to remember our Pledge of Allegiance, which celebrates "one nation, under God, indivisible." When political leaders attack any group within our nation—be it African-Americans, or Latino-Americans, or Muslim-Americans, or any other ethnicity or religion—we must reject the hate and bigotry and stand shoulder-to-shoulder with our fellow Americans.

And when it comes to those fleeing persecution and seeking refuge on our shores or borders, we need to treat them as we would want our family members to be treated, with respect and dignity as they apply for asylum. This does not mean that every refugee will meet the legal burden of proof required to win asylum. Far from it. But whether a refugee wins asylum or not, let him or her see a nation that recognizes the inherent dignity and value of all human beings, and treats each individual accordingly.

We must not let America dwell in the dark moral abyss in which we now reside. Martin Luther King said "Darkness cannot drive out darkness; only light can do that." Let's have more light. We must relight Lady Liberty's torch!

* * *

We must bring the nation together to restructure our child immigration system from top to bottom. A national commission producing a roadmap would be helpful. Such a commission should set the table for bipartisan deliberations in the House and Senate that can reset the national debate. Or let the House and Senate take this on directly. But let us not fail to deliberate and act.

We need to revamp every aspect of the system that is traumatizing the children fleeing to our country looking for safety: their experiences at the border; the process of applying for asylum; the system of sponsors for children awaiting asylum hearings; the child-prison facilities; and programs in the Northern Triangle.

Starting at the border, the first order of business should be to end metering and the border blockade. It is inhumane to push children back into Mexico and force them to choose between surviving in dangerous cities or crossing the border illegally. CBP officers, instead of blocking access by children, should provide immediate assistance and treat the children with respect. Each migrant child's first memory of stepping across the border should be of a smile, a warm greeting, a cold bottle of water, and some good snacks.

The *hieleras* have to go. Every facility should be a comfortable temperature, not cooled to make immigrants freeze through their detention on concrete benches and floors. And every child should get a basic medical evaluation within an hour of crossing the border whether at or between ports of entry. If a child has medical warning signs, we need to upgrade medical attention to a clinic or hospital immediately. Never again should a child like Jakelin or Felipe die in our care and custody.

Next, let's improve and streamline the asylum process. From day one the migrant child should be assigned a case worker and legal representation. The goal should be to get that child into a home with a sponsor expeditiously. Not only is this much better for the child's mental health, it saves a lot of money.

Immediate assignment of a legal advisor would also have a big impact. Every unaccompanied migrant child has the legal right to a non-adversarial asylum conference, but the process for arranging that conference is complicated, including filing an I-589 asylum application. To make this happen in a reasonable amount of time, a child needs an immigration advocate or lawyer so the conference can authentically consider all the relevant information that bears on the child's case. We should never again see images of toddlers supposedly "representing themselves" in immigration proceedings.

Children who arrive with their family are not eligible for the asylum conference but instead have their status determined through an asylum hearing for the family conducted by the Department of Justice. Every effort should be made to streamline and expedite this process as well. Families need to be assigned legal representation if they can't afford it themselves, and the asylum hearing should be scheduled within a modest number of months. Families need enough time to prepare their case, but no one benefits from years of delay.

Currently, there is a backlog of 800,000 immigration hearings. This is absurd. It generates years of delay in the conduct of asylum hearings. It is a solvable problem. We hire more judges. The cost of hiring those judges and support staff is a modest investment in the context of our overall immigration system.

Another factor that would greatly improve the asylum process is the system-wide use of case management once children or families are placed with a sponsor. Case management largely solves the problem in which migrants fail to show up for their check-ins or asylum hearings. It is also much less expensive than prisons. Holding 3,200 children—the capacity of Homestead as of April 2019—for a year costs about $875 million, as compared to $23 million for case management.

The system of sponsors is also ripe for reform. The most powerful immediate action to increase the supply of sponsors is to definitively end the procedure of sharing sponsors' applications with ICE. In addition, it makes sense to eliminate arbitrary requirements on potential sponsors like moving to a better community, or making more income, or renting a bigger house. If the issue isn't directly related to the safety and welfare of the child, the emphasis should be on quickly moving children out of prisons and detention centers and into homes, schools, and playgrounds.

We need to identify and fix the chokepoints in this system. If more caseworkers, or federal field specialists, or fingerprint teams are needed, let's hire them. If a sponsor can be identified as a relative and there is no criminal record, then let's do away with the fingerprinting altogether. As for children who don't have relatives, let's open up sponsorship to other families with appropriate vetting. I can't tell you how many families I've met in Oregon who have said that they would be happy to sponsor a child in their home.

Now let's turn to reform in the network of child prisons. A good place to start is to take seriously the spirit behind the Flores Settlement Agreement, and deliver children to state-licensed care facilities within 72 hours even during periods of "influx." Twenty days is far too long for children to be locked up in a prison. If more resources are needed, let's spend them on state-licensed facilities, not fabulously expensive and less appropriate unlicensed temporary prisons.

Another important reform is to eliminate for-profit child prisons. There is no way that a for-profit company can adequately resolve the conflict between their responsibility to move children quickly into state-licensed care facilities and sponsors' homes and their desire to increase their profits by keeping more children locked up for longer periods.

We should also end child mega-prisons. Facilities like Tornillo, Homestead, and Casa Padre that hold more than a thousand children make no sense. There is no way children can get the kind of attention and support they need in facilities that size. ORR should not place children in facilities holding more than 100 children.

And every facility, regardless of size, should be open to a congressional visit on short notice. No member of Congress is going to get an honest sense of how a facility is operating if ORR has two weeks to polish everything up. To exercise real oversight, members should be able to get a guided tour of a child prison or detention center with 24 to 48 hours of notice.

Finally, we need to seriously examine our programs in the Northern Triangle. We should thoroughly evaluate which programs work most effectively and fund them aggressively. If, for example, school lunches are one of the most powerful ways to tackle both education and nutrition as President Morales suggested, we should greatly amplify that program in close coordination with the government of Guatemala. What would it take to get an effective lunch program into every remote village?

We should recognize that our current investment in the region is small. We fund the U.S. Strategy in Central America at significantly less than $1 billion per year, which is dwarfed by the $17 billion in remittances sent to the Northern Triangle from the United States in 2018. And our investment is small compared to the enormous sums we are spending on border security. If the U.S. strategy to help rebuild the Northern Triangle is going to work, we are going to have to invest far more.

We also should consider new approaches. Is there a way to make it much harder for drug money to be laundered and passed back to the Northern Triangle? Is there a way, perhaps in partnership with Mexico, to make it difficult for guns to flow from the U.S. to the region? Would gun buybacks reduce murders? Can we persuade the three nations to have a more progressive tax system and more effective tax collection to support programs that improve life for ordinary residents? Does it make sense to tax remittances and invest the proceeds directly on the ground in those nations? If given assistance, can other towns replicate the experience of San José Guayabal in El Salvador, where citizens have taken their town back from the gangs? Let's bring in all the experts in the region and test out the most promising ideas.

* * *

Perhaps more important than any set of policy proposals for reforming our child immigration system is the challenge of having the right fundamental values as the foundation for the system. One of the values should be to never intentionally harm children, and to treat each child with respect and dignity as he or she moves through an expedited asylum process.

And there is a bigger issue to consider, which is to ask ourselves who we are. How have we slid backward to the point that we stranded children in Mexico, held them in *hieleras*, locked them up in mega-prisons, and treated them as pawns in a political strategy rather than as people. America is a special place, and part of our specialness has been the determination to give every child the opportunity to thrive and to set a standard for fair treatment and human rights that is an inspiration to the world. Those qualities have made us a stronger, better nation, earned us well-deserved respect, and made the world a better place.

That promise of America as a place of fair treatment and opportunity is important to me. After all, I grew up hearing about my grandmother who hand-washed laundry to survive and had to surrender her first three children to the

county because of stark poverty; and here I am, two generations later, serving in the Senate. As a nation, we've never
fully delivered on the promise of fairness and opportunity
for all, to be sure, but we have been striving toward that
ideal, and making progress generation after generation. That
promise of fairness and freedom and opportunity is why
those immigrants on the ships waved at Lady Liberty. Heck,
it's why they got on those ships in the first place and left
behind everyone and everything they knew.

The scandal of child separation profoundly disturbed me
and so many people across the country both because it is
wrong, unacceptable under any moral code or religious tra-
dition. But it also disturbs us because it undermines our own
sense of ourselves—and of America—as champions for fairness, and freedom, and opportunity. As such champions, we
should be protecting the vulnerable from those who would
prey on them. We should give the people in the toughest circumstances the tools they need to lift themselves up. And
there is no group more vulnerable and in need of a champion
than children fleeing for their lives from violence, who come
to a new country looking for safety.

Now is the time for some self-reflection. Our failure to
protect migrant children is a poignant and emotional challenge to the vision of our nation as a champion for fairness,
freedom, and opportunity—not just for migrant children,
but for anyone without power and status.

We have a choice. We can fight to renew the values of fairness, freedom, and opportunity that will drive innovation

and growth and inspire the world, or we can pull up the ladders, circle the wagons, and fight over who gets the biggest share of what our parents and previous generations have built. We need to decide if our most powerful founding ideal of opportunity for everyone is to be tossed on the scrapheap of history, or reinvigorated as a driving animating force for a better nation and better world yet to come.

* * *

It was a great joy to have Albertina and Yaquelin Contreras as my guests at President Trump's State of the Union speech in 2019. They had come to give voice to the brutality of Trump's policies of child separation and imprisonment on behalf of all the children who have been and will be injured by it.

In a twist of fate, Yaquelin was celebrating her 12th birthday that evening. After all she had suffered—from the journey to the border to the forced separation from her mother—we wanted her to feel special. My team decorated our conference room with birthday greetings. There was a Happy Birthday sign hanging in one corner and a giant card saying, FELIZ CUMPLEAÑOS, YAQUELIN! We had cupcakes for everyone, and one festooned with candles for Yaquelin herself. With my Oregon office joining in by video link, we all sang "Happy Birthday" in Spanish and gave her a huge birthday card along with gifts for the birthday girl and her mother.

"You have a large family that is cheering you on as you start your new life," I told Yaquelin. "And in your new neighborhood we want you to have a bike." We had heard that that was something she really wanted.

"Thank you so much from my heart," said Albertina on behalf of both of them and looking a little dazed. "You have really big and beautiful hearts. I feel so full of happiness. Thank you."

A little later, we took the small subway train from the basement of my Senate office building to the basement of the Capitol. Yaquelin and Albertina were excited to sit in the front seat. We rushed through the new visitor center on our way to a special dinner for members of Congress and their guests before the speech itself. Suddenly I found myself walking ahead on my own: They had stopped to stare through a skylight at the Capitol dome glowing bright against a deep purple sky, colored by the final touch of the setting sun.

All evening Yaquelin was a charming teenager, who smiled through every question that came her way. Her mother seemed much more solemn. I had the strong sense that she had seen and experienced things that are a heavy burden to carry. And she still has two sons back in Guatemala she misses greatly. It was hard to know what they were really thinking through the dinner and the speech that followed, which was full of Trump's familiar tactics of characterizing immigrants as murderers and thugs.

After the speech, they seemed exhausted by the day and we slogged our way through several media interviews. I tried to keep their spirits up with the little Spanish I could remember, including teaching Yaquelin the song "De Colores," which I was taught by a child in Mexico. It's a beautiful song that celebrates the colors of the fields in the springtime, the colors of the rainbow, and the colors of the little birds that fly in from afar. That's what children should be doing—singing and celebrating the beauty of the world, not suffering behind bars.

As we finished up, we walked past the giant white figure of Freedom—the plaster model used to cast the bronze statue that sits on top of the Capitol dome. They perked up when they heard its name, *Libertad*, and posed for photos in front of it.

On the walk back through the basement hallways, we bumped into Senator Mazie Hirono from Hawaii. "I'm an immigrant, too," she said. "I'm the only immigrant in the Senate. My mother raised me to work hard," she added with a warm smile, looking at Yaquelin. When Senator Hirono's mother emigrated to escape violence in Japan, she had to leave a child behind, just as Albertina had to do.

"I just want to keep moving, not going backwards," Yaquelin told me. "Because here in the United States, there are lots of opportunities, and there aren't so many back home."

"I would like, with all my heart and strength, to stay in the United States," said her mother, Albertina. "I want to bring my children here that I left behind."

You would be hard pressed to find two people further removed from the dismal image of immigrants that Donald Trump had just conjured up in a speech televised across the nation. They didn't deserve their suffering in Guatemala, and they didn't deserve their suffering in the United States.

Whatever happens in their asylum hearing, they had caught a glimpse of the better life that everyone surely deserves.

May we not forget the message that Albertina and Yaquelin came to deliver that day: that no child or family should ever be intentionally hurt through child separation or extended imprisonment.

America is better than this.

ACKNOWLEDGMENTS

This project would not have been possible without the support of **Mary Sorteberg**. I'm the luckiest man alive to have met her 31 years ago when my roommate invited her to dinner. She has backed me up through projects large and small over the decades, and without her love and encouragement, few of them would have made it off the drawing board. She has been an amazing partner in the raising of our two beautiful children, **Jonathan** and **Brynne**, who are hard at work finding their own paths to building a better world.

My entire Senate staff fights tirelessly and effectively for a nation that will treat every person with dignity and create opportunity for all to thrive. I owe special thanks to those on the team who have worked on immigration in many capacities: scheduling and staffing trips, consulting experts, drafting legislation, and writing press releases and speeches. None of my work to shine a light on the Trump administration's treatment of migrant families would have happened without members of my policy team, including **Matt Traylor, Meredith Booker,** and **Lauren Oppenheimer;** Oregon team members who organized and staffed the visit to Sheridan Prison including **Jessica Stevens, Stacey Jochimsen,** and **Amy Bacher;** Constituent Services Representative **Whitney Navarro Castillo,** who specializes in immigration issues; my communications team of **Ray Zaccaro, Martina McLennan, Sara Hottman,** and **Mike McKiernan;** and my administrative team members **Jennifer Piorkowski, Carly Vandegrift** and **Michael Zamore,** my Chief of Staff who coordinates the efforts of an extraordinary team. I am privileged to work in the company of such capable and dedicated individuals.

I am deeply indebted to the many advocates who provided briefings on immigration issues. **Jennifer Harbury** and **Michael Seifert** of the ACLU of Texas provided insights on my first trip to the McAllen border processing station and Casa Padre in Brownsville. A huge thanks to **Ruben Garcia** and **Taylor Levy** of Annunciation House, which has provided critical services to refugees left on their doorstep.

Shaw Drake and **Cynthia Pompa** of the ACLU Texas Border Rights Center graciously briefed our congressional delegation on a Saturday morning before we visited Tornillo. **Joshua Rubin** planted himself outside Tornillo for months and helped people understand what was going on from his view at the front gate. **Kevin Dinnin,** CEO of BCFS, hosted our delegation inside the gates at Tornillo and gave his forthright understanding of the workings of the influx prison and the broader system. **Jennifer Anzardo Valdes** and **Michelle M. Ortiz** of Americans for Immigrant Justice, Inc. provided insights on the operation of Homestead.

Shay Fluharty introduced me to Elena and Carolina and has provided critical legal assistance to innumerable families through her work at the Dilley Pro Bono Project. **Andrea Meza** with the Refugee and Immigrant Center for Education and Legal Services (RAICES) has been a valuable resource regarding the operations at Karnes Family Detention Center. **Dr. Scott Allen**, who works with the Department of Homeland Security Office of Civil Rights and Civil Liberties provided essential context on both Dilley and Karnes.

I'm grateful to attorney **Andrew Free** and his associate **Marlee Deck**, who provided pro bono legal assistance to Yaquelin and Albertina Contreras; and thanks goes to **Katie Shepherd**, with the Immigration Justice Campaign, who assisted with the Contreras' trip to President Trump's 2019 State of the Union address.

Erika Pinheiro, Nicole Ramos, and **Luis Guerra** of Al Otro Lado and their volunteer **Eric Hill-Tanquist** provided extensive insight into the U.S. border blockade for migrants seeking asylum, including the use of metering. Many thanks to the U.S. Consul General in Tijuana, **Sue Saarnio**, and the Vice Counsel, **Genevieve Judson-Jourdain**, who arranged for Congressman Correa and me to visit seven shelters in Tijuana and El Chaparral on the border. I appreciated our tour guides for the shelters in Tijuana including **Tim Kilcoyne**, Director of Chef Operations, World Central Kitchen; pastor

Alberto Rivera Colón, who gave us a tour of AGAPE Misión Mundial; Leticia Herrera, Director of Una Luz de Esperanza; and Hector Barajas-Varela, founder of Deported Vets Support House, also known as "the bunker."

Many, many thanks to Senator Tom Carper for organizing a congressional delegation to the Northern Triangle and including me in it. The State Department diplomats and personnel did a marvelous job organizing our meetings with the government and community leaders of Guatemala, Honduras, and El Salvador. Several experts provided excellent briefings before the trip, including Wendy Young, President, Kids in Need of Defense and Matt Clausen and Adriana Beltrán of the Washington Office on Latin America. And a special thanks both to the founders of Child Aid, Richard Carroll and Nancy Press, who have built an extraordinary program to provide books and train teachers in Guatemala, and to the Child Aid leaders who met with me on site on short notice: Graciela Pichiya, National Program Director; Jeremias Morales, Senior Supervisor; and Andres Galvez, Board Member.

I received assistance on the nuances of the Flores Settlement Agreement from Neha Desai, Director of Immigration at the National Center for Youth Law, and Peter Schey, Executive Director of the Center for Human Rights & Constitutional Law. Eric Schwartz, President of Refugees International (RI), and Yael Schacher, RI Senior U.S. Domestic Advocate, provided extensive and valuable comments on a draft of the book.

ACKNOWLEDGMENTS

Special appreciation goes to the many members of Congress who are standing up against the strategy of abusing migrant children, including the Congressional Hispanic Caucus, which graciously included me in their delegation to Texas and New Mexico to explore both the deficiencies in healthcare for migrant children broadly and the deaths of the first two children who perished in U.S. custody.

This book would never have gotten off the ground without an excellent production team. **Gail Ross** guided me through the process as my agent extraordinaire. **Sean Desmond** with Twelve Publishing shaped the vision and greenlighted the project. And I am most indebted to **Richard Wolffe**, who prompted me to illuminate the complicated issues of immigration with the stories of ordinary migrants in search of a better life. He worked diligently to structure the first draft and to refine each subsequent iteration. If you find any particularly poetic turn of phrase in this volume, credit goes to Richard. And the project benefitted from the assistance of **Pamela Sharma**, who signed on as a research assistant and helped out time and again at critical moments, even as she was preparing for finals and graduation from college.

And finally, thank you to the millions of Americans who have written, called, protested, donated, posted on social media, and otherwise raised their voices to challenge the terrible policies described in this book. You are not only standing up for the children and families seeking refuge in our country, you are standing up for our country—for the better America we should be.

NOTES

Prologue: The Most Cruel Law

1. The spelling of the name of Albertina's daughter has varied in different articles. The spelling used here, "Yaquelin," is the spelling she prefers.
2. Manny Fernandez, " 'You Have to Pay with Your Body': The Hidden Nightmare of Sexual Violence on the Border," *New York Times*, March 3, 2019, https://www.nytimes.com/2019/03/03/us/border-rapes-migrant-women.html.

One: Child Separation

1. U.S. Department of Justice, "Attorney General Sessions Delivers Remarks Discussing the Immigration Enforcement Actions of the Trump Administration," San Diego, California, May 7, 2018, https://www.justice.gov/opa/speech/attorney-general-sessions-delivers-remarks-discussing-immigration-enforcement-actions.

2. U.S. Department of Homeland Security, Office of Inspector General, "Special Review—Initial Observations Regarding Family Separation Issues Under the Zero Tolerance Policy," September 27, 2018, https://www.oig.dhs.gov /reports/2018/special-review-initial-observations-regard ing-family-separation-issues-under-zero-tolerance -policy/oig-18-84-sep18.

3. Maya Rhodan, "Sen. Jeff Merkley: 'Zero Tolerance' Refugee Policy Is Actually 'Zero Humanity'" *Time*, June 4, 2018.

4. Ali Rogin and Gina Sunseri "Police called as Sen. Jeff Merkley tries to enter immigrant children's shelter," ABC News, June 5, 2018.

5. Ted Hesson, "White House blasts Merkley after his attempt to visit a shelter for migrant children," *Politico*, June 4, 2018.

6. Donald Trump, tweet at 7:58 a.m., June 5, 2018, https://twit ter.com/realDonaldTrump/status/1003969399148118016.

7. Betsy Klein, "Melania Dons Jacket Saying 'I Really Don't Care. Do U?' Ahead of Her Border Visit—and Afterward," CNN, June 21, 2018, https://www.cnn.com /2018/06/21/politics/melania-trump-jacket/index.html.

Two: Zero Tolerance

1. Julia Edwards Ainsley, "Exclusive: Trump Administration Considering Separating Women, Children at Mexican Border," Reuters, March 3, 2017, https://www.reuters

.com/article/us-usa-immigration-children-idUSKBN16 A2ES.

2. Ibid.

3. Ibid.

4. Dr. Frank Luntz, "The Language of Health care 2009: The 10 Rules for Stopping the Washington Takeover of Healthcare," politico.com/pdf/PPM116_luntz.pdf.

5. Bill Adair and Angie Drobnic Holan, "PolitiFact's Lie of the Year: 'A government takeover of health care,'" Politi-Fact, December 16, 2010.

6. Daniella Diaz, "Kelly: DHS Is Considering Separating Undocumented Children from Their Parents at the Border," CNN, March 7, 2017, https://www.cnn.com /2017/03/06/politics/john-kelly-separating-children -from-parents-immigration-border/index.html.

7. Interview, The Situation Room, March 6, 2017.

8. U.S. Department of Homeland Security, "Home and Away: DHS and the Threats to America, Remarks Delivered by Secretary Kelly at George Washington University Center for Cyber and Homeland Security," April 18, 2017, https://www.dhs.gov/news/2017/04/18/home-and -away-dhs-and-threats-america.

9. Alana Abramson, "'They Aren't People.' President Trump Calls Deported Gang Members 'Animals,'" Time, May 16, 2018.

10. U.S. Department of Health and Human Services, Office of Inspector General, "Separated Children Placed in

Office of Refugee Resettlement Care," January 17, 2019, https://oig.hhs.gov/oei/reports/oei-BL-18-00511.asp.

11. Katie Benner and Caitlin Dickerson, "Sessions Says Domestic and Gang Violence Are Not Grounds for Asylum," *New York Times*, June 11, 2018, https://www.nytimes.com/2018/06/11/us/politics/sessions-domestic-violence-asylum.html.

12. Walter A. Ewing, Ph.D., Daniel E. Martinez, Ph.D., and Rubén G. Rumbaut, Ph.D. *Special Report: The Criminalization of Immigration in the United States*, American Immigration Council, July 2015.

13. 2014 Mexican National Survey of Demographics Dynamics, https://www.pewhispanic.org/2015/11/19/more-mexicans-leaving-than-coming-to-the-u-s/.

14. Benner and Dickerson, "Sessions Says."

15. U.S. Department of Justice, Office of the Attorney General, "Matter of A-B-, Respondent, Decided by Attorney General June 11, 2018," June 11, 2018, https://www.justice.gov/eoir/page/file/1070866/download.

16. Benner and Dickerson, "Sessions Says."

17. Ibid.

18. "Central Americans Were Increasingly Winning Asylum Before President Trump Took Office," Human Rights First fact sheet, January 2019.

19. "Grace v. Whitaker," ACLU.org, January 10, 2019.

20. "Catholic Bishops Issue Scathing Statement on Trump's Family Separation Policy," CBS News, June 14, 2018,

https://www.cbsnews.com/news/catholic-bishops-statement-on-trump-immigration-policies-family-separation-border/.

21. Rebecca Shabad, "Pelosi: Trump administration policy separating parents and children at border 'barbaric,'" NBC News, June 14, 2018.

22. Laurie Goodstein, "Conservative Religious Leaders Are Denouncing Trump Immigration Policies," *New York Times*, June 14, 2018, https://www.nytimes.com/2018/06/14/us/trump-immigration-religion.html.

23. United States Department of Justice, "Attorney General Sessions Addresses Recent Criticisms of Zero Tolerance by Church Leaders" Fort Wayne, IN; June 14, 2018, https://www.justice.gov/opa/speech/attorney-general-sessions-addresses-recent-criticisms-zero-tolerance-church-leaders.

24. Ibid.

25. "Results of Unannounced Inspections of Conditions for Unaccompanied Alien Children in CBP Custody" September 28, 2018, OIG-18-87.

26. Julia Edwards Ainsley, "Former ICE Director: Some Migrant Family Separations Are Permanent," NBC News, June 19, 2018, https://www.nbcnews.com/storyline/immigration-border-crisis/former-ice-director-some-migrant-family-separations-are-permanent-n884391.

27. Julia Edwards Ainsley, "Exclusive: Trump administration considering separating women, children at Mexico border," March 3, 2017.

28. Dartunorro Clark, " 'I Am Not a Liar': DHS Chief Nielsen Defends Immigration Policies in Heated Hearing," NBC News, December 20, 2018, https://www.nbcnews.com /politics/congress/i-am-not-liar-dhs-chief-nielsen -defends-immigration-policies-n950511.

29. National Public Radio, "Transcript: White House Chief of Staff John Kelly's Interview with NPR" May 11, 2018.

30. Ted Hesson, "Memo shows DHS considered stepped -up family separations in 2017." *Politico*, January 18, 2019.

31. Miriam Jordan and Caitlin Dickerson, "U.S. Continues to Separate Migrant Families Despite Rollback of Policy," *New York Times*, March 9, 2019.

Three: Zero Humanity

1. Scott A. Allen and Pamela McPherson, "We Warned DHS That a Migrant Child Could Die in U.S. Custody. Now One Has," *Washington Post*, December 19, 2018.

2. Sofia Menchú and José Alejandro García, " 'I'm in Despair': A Mother and Village Mourn Guatemalan Boy's Death in US," the *Guardian*, December 29, 2018, https://www .theguardian.com/world/2018/dec/29/felipe-gomez -alonzo-guatemala-boy-death-us-custody-home-village -mourns.

3. Zolan Kanno-Youngs, "Guatemalan Boy Dies in U.S. Custody After Illness, Officials Say," *New York Times,* May, 1, 2019.

4. Julie M. Linton, Marsha Griffin, Alan J. Shapiro, Council on Community Pediatrics, "Detention of Immigrant Children," *Pediatrics*, May 2017 (Volume 139/Issue 5).

5. Jody Berger, "A Look Inside the Child Detention Centers Near the U.S. Border," *Scope* (blog), Stanford Medicine, September 17, 2018.

6. Miriam Jordan, "A Migrant Boy Rejoins His Mother But He's Not the Same," *New York Times*, 7/31/18. https://www.nytimes.com/2018/07/31/us/migrant-children-separation-anxiety.html.

7. Linton et al., "Detention of Immigrant Children."

8. Maria Sacchetti, "Top Homeland Security officials urge criminal prosecution of parents crossing border with children," *Washington Post*, April 26, 2018, https://www.washingtonpost.com/local/immigration/top-homeland-security-officials-urge-criminal-prosecution-of-parents-who-cross-border-with-children/2018/04/26/a0bdcee0-4964-11e8-8b5a-3b1697adcc2a_story.html?utm_term=.9e48019d62cb.

9. Jordan, "A Migrant Boy."

10. Ibid.

11. Attorney General of Texas, Custodial Death Report 18-449-CJ, June 5, 2018, https://oagtx.force.com/cdr/VIPForm_VIP_FormWizardPDF?id=a2Ct000000YtXkEAK.

12. Jeffrey C. Mays and Matt Stevens, "Honduran Man Kills Himself After Being Separated From Family at U.S. Border, Reports Say," *New York Times*, June 10, 2018,

https://www.nytimes.com/2018/06/10/us/border-patrol
-texas-family-separated-suicide.html.

Four: Reunification

1. "Mother separated from child in immigrant detention,"
   Associated Press, March 6, 2018.
2. Ms. L.; et al., v. U.S. Immigration and Customs Enforcement ("ICE"); et al., Order Granting Plaintiffs' Motion
   for Classwide Preliminary Injunction, U.S. District Court,
   Southern District of California, June 26, 2018, https://
   int.nyt.com/data/documenthelper/58-federal-judge
   -rules-on-immigra/425f7ff96a5dcb98ecce/optimized
   /full.pdf#page=1.
3. Geneva Sands and Lauren Pearle, "Trump administration misses court deadline to reunited separated children
   with their parents," ABC News, July 11, 2018.
4. Marisa Schultz, "HHS Secretary says he can find separated migrant kids 'within seconds,'" *New York Post*,
   June 26, 2018.
5. Nick Miroff, Amy Goldstein and Maria Sacchetti,
   " 'Deleted' families: What went wrong with Trump's family-
   separation effort," *Washington Post*, July 28, 2018, https://
   www.washingtonpost.com/local/social-issues/deleted
   -families-what-went-wrong-with-trumps-family
   -separation-effort/2018/07/28/54bcdcc6-90cb-11e8-8322
   -b5482bf5eof5_story.html?utm_term=.21f8f53eb757.

6. Ron Nixon, "U.S. Loses Track of Another 1,500 Migrant Children, Investigators Find," *New York Times*, September 18, 2018, https://www.nytimes.com/2018/09/18/us/politics/us-migrant-children-whereabouts-.html.

7. Leila Miller, "HHS Official Says Agency Lost Track of Nearly 1,500 Unaccompanied Minors," *Frontline*, April 26, 2018, https://www.pbs.org/wgbh/frontline/article/hhs-official-says-agency-lost-track-of-nearly-1500-unaccompanied-minors/.

8. Camila DeChalus, "New Bill Would Hold HHS Feet to Fire for Unaccompanied Minors," *Roll Call*, September 21, 2018, https://www.rollcall.com/news/politics/new-bill-hold-hhs-feet-fire-unaccompanied-minors.

9. Michael D. Shear, Julie Hirschfeld Davis, Thomas Kaplan, and Robert Pear, "Federal Judge in California Halts Splitting of Migrant Families at Border," *New York Times*, June 26, 2018, https://www.nytimes.com/2018/06/26/us/politics/family-separations-congress-states.html.

10. Tal Kopan, "Judge slams Trump admin for suggesting ACLU, others should find deported parents," CNN.com, August 3, 2018, https://www.cnn.com/2018/08/03/politics/trump-administration-aclu-deported-parents/index.html.

11. "A Honduran father is reunited with his daughter, 10 months after being separated," NPR, March 14, 2019.

12. Letter from Senators Masto and Merkley, et al, March 26, 2019, https://www.cortezmasto.senate.gov/imo/media

/doc/Cortez%20Masto%20Letter%20to%20DHS%20
re%20Reuniting%20Separated%20Families.pdf.

13. William Cummings, "It may take 2 years to identify thousands of migrant children separated from families," *USA
Today*, April 7, 2019, https://www.usatoday.com/story
/news/politics/2019/04/07/immigration-family-separations
-may-take-2-years-identify-children/3393536002/.

Five: Internment Camps

1. Michael D. Shear, Abby Goodnough and Maggie Haberman, "Trump Retreats on Separating Families, but Thousands May Remain Apart," *New York Times*, June 20, 2018,
https//www.nytimes.com/2018/06/20/us/politics/trump
-immigration-children-executive-order.html.

2. "Affording Congress an Opportunity to Address Family
Separation," Executive Order 13841, June 20, 2018, https://
www.govinfo.gov/content/pkg/FR-2018-06-25/pdf
/2018-13696.pdf.

3. "Policy and Legal Experts Respond to Trump's Executive Order," America's Voice, June 20,2018, https://
americasvoice.org/press_releases/policy-and-legal
-experts-respond-to-trumps-executive-order/.

4. Ibid.

5. "Affording Congress an Opportunity to Address Family Separation," Executive Order 13841, June 20, 2018,
available at https://www.govinfo.gov/content/pkg/FR
-2018-06-25/pdf/2018-13696.pdf.

6. Rebeca M. López, "Codifying the *Flores* Settlement Agreement: Seeking to Protect Immigrant Children in U.S. Custody," *Marquette Law Review* 95, no. 4 (Summer 2012): 1637–51, https://scholarship.law.marquette.edu/cgi/viewcontent.cgi?referer=https://www.cnn.com/2018/07/10/politics/flores-settlement-history/index.html&httpsredir=1&article=5138&context=mulr.

7. Stipulated Settlement Agreement, Flores v. Reno, Case No. CV 85-4544-RJK(Px), January 17, 1997 (C.D. Ca.), https://www.aclu.org/legal-document/flores-v-meese-stipulated-settlement-agreement-plus-extension-settlement.

8. Case No. CV 85-4544 DMG, June 27, 2017, Jenny L. Flores, et al. v. Jefferson B. Sessions, III, et al.

9. Nick Miroff, Josh Dawsey, and Maria Sacchetti, "Trump Administration Weighs New Family Separation Effort at Border," *Washington Post*, October 12, 2018.

10. "Apprehension, Processing, Care, and Custody of Alien Minors and Unaccompanied Alien Children." A Proposed Rule by the Homeland Security Department and the Health and Human Services Department on September 7, 2018.

11. The High Costs of the Proposed *Flores* Regulation, By Philip E. Wolgin Posted on October 19, 2018.

12. Ibid.

13. Michael D. Shear, Abby Goodnough, and Maggie Haberman, "Trump Retreats on Separating Families, but Thousands May Remain Apart," *New York Times*, 6/20/18.

14. https://twitter.com/chuckgrassley/status/10072892702 96629248?lang=en.

15. HR 6136

16. Calendar No. 497; 115th Congress, 2d Session; Senate Report 115-289; Departments of Labor, Health and Human Services, and Education, and Related Agencies Appropriation Bill, 2019; June 28, 2018.

17. Family Case Management Program (FCMP) Close-Out Report, U.S. Immigration and Customs Enforcement, February 2018.

18. Ibid.

19. Department of Homeland Security, U.S. Immigration and Customs Enforcement Budget Overview, Fiscal Year 2019, Congressional Justification, p. 111.

20. United States Government Accountability Office, "Alternatives to Detention: Improved Data Collection and Analyses Needed to Better Assess Program Effectiveness," November 2014. https://www.gao.gov/assets/670/666911.pdf.

Six: American Gulag

1. The years in this paragraph are based on federal fiscal years, which run from October 1 through September 30; the statistics are from the Office of Refugee Resettlement, https://www.acf.hhs.gov/orr/about/ucs/facts-and-data.

2. Julia Ainsley and Annie Rose Ramos, "Inside Tornillo: The Expanded Tent City for Migrant Children," NBC

News, October 12, 2018, https://www.nbcnews.com/politics/immigration/inside-tornillo-expanded-tent-city-migrant-children-n919431.

3. Garance Burke and Martha Mendoza, "Texas Detention Camp for Teen Migrants Keeps Growing," Associated Press, November 27, 2018, https://www.apnews.com/16f53fb6dd644662a1e52bbad72d99cc.

4. "Desert Detention Camp For Migrant Kids Still Growing," Associated Press, November 27, 2018.

5. Edwin Delgado, "Tornillo: Detention Site for Migrant Children to Close Amid Safety Fears," *Guardian*, January 12, 2019.

6. "Company Behind Florida Migrant Children Camp Drops IPO Plans," *US News and World Report*, March 5, 2019.

7. Tal Kopan, "Immigrant children in US custody soaring back toward record levels," *San Franciso Chronicle*, May 10, 2019, https://www.sfchronicle.com/politics/article/Immigrant-children-in-US-custody-soaring-back-13834123.php?psid=4yMwl.

8. Michael E. Miller, Emma Brown, and Aaron C. Davis, "Inside Casa Padre, the Converted Walmart Where the U.S. Is Holding Nearly 1,500 Immigrant Children," *Washington Post*, June 14, 2018.

9. Ibid.

10. Kim Barker, Nicholas Kulish, and Rebecca R. Ruiz, "He's Built an Empire, with Detained Migrant Children as the Bricks," *New York Times*, December 2, 2018, https://

www.nytimes.com/2018/12/02/us/southwest-key
-migrant-children.html.

11. Jay Root, "Juan Sanchez Stepping Down as CEO of South-west Key Programs," *Texas Tribune*, March 11, 2019, https://www.texastribune.org/2019/03/11/juan-sanchez
-stepping-down-ceo-southwest-key-programs/.

12. "Deutch Releases Data Showing Sexual Assault of Unaccompanied Minors in HHS Custody," Office of Rep. Ted Deutch, February 26, 2019, https://teddeutch.house.gov/news/documentsingle.aspx?DocumentID=399520.

13. Senator Charles Grassley and Senator Dianne Feinstein to Daniel R. Levinson, February 28, 2019, https://www.grassley.senate.gov/sites/default/files/2019-02-28%20DF%2C%20Grassley%20to%20HHS%20OIG%20-%20Sexual%20Abuse%20in%20HHS%20Facilities 0.pdf

14. Laura Gómez, "Migrant Youth Shelter Reform Bill Approved in Senate," *AZ Mirror*, February 28, 2019, https://www.azmirror.com/blog/migrant-youth-shelter
-reform-bill-approved-in-senate/.

Eight: The Misery Triangle

1. Mandalit Del Barco, "The International Reach of the Mara Salvatrucha," NPR, March 17, 2005, https://www.npr.org/2005/03/17/4539688/the-international
-reach-of-the-mara-salvatrucha.

2. Joe Biden, "A Plan for Central America," *New York Times*, January 29, 2015, https://www.nytimes.com/2015/01/30/opinion/joe-biden-a-plan-for-central-america.html.

3. "International homicides (per 100,000 people)," The World Bank.

4. World Politics Review; "El Salvador's 'Iron Fist': Inside Its Unending War on Gangs," Christine Wade, Monday, June 6, 2016; InSight Crime, "How 'Mano Dura' Is Strengthening Gangs," Steven Dudley, November 22, 2010.

5. Agence France Presse (AFP); "El Salvador's 'vigilante' mayor battling the gangs," November 29, 2018.

6. Ibid.

7. Colum Lynch, "Corrupt Guatemalans' GOP Lifeline," *Foreign Policy*, February 5, 2019, https://foreignpolicy.com/2019/02/05/trump-republican-lawmakers-weaken-u-n-anti-corruption-commission-guatemala-jimmy-morales-white-house-putin/.

8. Elisabeth Malkin, "Guatemala Corruption Panel Has New Foe: U.S. Senator Marco Rubio," *New York Times*, May 6, 2018, https://www.nytimes.com/2018/05/06/world/americas/guatemala-corruption-marco-rubio.html.

Nine: Border Blockade

1. The U.S. Government Turned Away Thousands of Jewish Refugees, Fearing That They Were Nazi Spies; Daniel A. Gross; smithsonian.com, November 18, 2015.

2. "Special Review–Initial Observations Regarding Family Separation Issues Under the Zero Tolerance Policy," Office of the Inspector General, Department of Homeland Security, September 27, 2018, OIG-18-84.

3. ACLU Border Rights; "Port Monitoring Initial Findings," March 2019.

4. Kate Morrissey "Unaccompanied children stuck in Tijuana, hoping to reach U.S.," *San Diego Union-Tribune*, March 31, 2019.

5. Kate Morrissey, "Unaccompanied children."

6. Emily Green, "Two migrant teens brutally executed in Tijuana as asylum cases pile up," Vice News, January 3, 2019.

7. ACLU Border Rights; "Port Monitoring Initial Findings," March 2019.

8. Kate Morrissey, "Unaccompanied children."

9. U.S. Code Title 8, Section 1158. Asylum. http://uscode .house.gov/view.xhtml?req=granuleid%3AUSC-prelim -title8-section1158&num=0&edition=prelim.

10. Kate Morrissey, "Scheduling Glitch Affects First Hearings for 'Remain in Mexico' Returnees," *San Diego Union-Tribune*, March 14, 2019, https://www.sandiegouniontribune.com /news/immigration/sd-me-remain-in-mexico-hearings -20190314-story.html.

11. Alan Gomez, "Judge Blocks Trump Policy Forcing Asylum-Seekers to Wait in Mexico," *USA Today*, April 8, 2019, https://www.usatoday.com/story/news/politics/2019

/04/08/judge-blocks-trump-policy-forcing-asylum-seekers
-wait-mexico/3244127002/.

12. Robert Moore, " 'I'm in Danger': Migrant Parents Face
Violence in Mexico Under New Trump Policy," *Texas
Monthly*, April 25, 2019.